## Praise for *Prodigal F[...]*

"The brutal candor of these exchanges [...]                                    son
caught in a vicious cycle of competition[...] ...prehension can be hard
to take. Stick with it. Both have hurt each other so much that reconciliation
comes hard. But what they prove in the end is that the statute of limitations
can run out on the wrong we do to one another. Every father and son, mother
and daughter, parent and child should exult in the Keens' discovery that it is
never too late to start over."
**—Bill Moyers**

"A courageous look at father-and-son struggles over the years. This universal
and archetypal [conflict] is the inheritance of us all. I identified with Sam,
and found insights about my son through Gifford's sharing. Their method of
reconciliation is a 'gift' for us all. Here is a raw human story that has a joyful
ending."
**—John Bradshaw, author of *Post-Romantic Stress Disorder: What to Do When
the Honeymoon Is Over***

"In this fine book, honest and eloquent pain spills across every page. This open-
hearted sharing is in the service of great teachings. Many fathers and sons will
read this and see a path forward."
**—Mary Pipher, author of *The Green Boat***

"*Prodigal Father, Wayward Son* is the most heart-opening book I have ever read.
On the surface, it is about virtually every dad and son. Beneath the surface, it
opened my heart to further removing the walls between myself and those I
yearn to more deeply love. Its fierce honesty and loving grace lead the way. Of
Sam Keen's many terrific books, this gets my vote for his best."
**—Warren Farrell, author of *Father and Child Reunion***

"Moving and inspiring; this groundbreaking book is the story of father and son
overcoming the broken bond of trust and love. Sam Keen, a most trusted voice
in our culture for 50 years, and his son Gifford, equally strong and compelling,
show a way through struggle and radical honesty that allows fathers and sons
to overcome long-festering estrangement and become the best of friends."
**—Linda Carroll, author of *Love Cycles***

"Sam and Gifford Keen embody the redemptive power of honest storytelling in their extraordinarily revealing book *Prodigal Father, Wayward Son*. This father/son relationship is transformed by telling many stories beyond the damaging ones that have kept them apart. The message of this book moves beyond fathers and sons to any intimate relationship that is controlled by a handful of old myths."

**—Herbert Anderson, coauthor of *Mighty Stories, Dangerous Rituals* and coauthor (with Karen Speerstra) of *The Divine Art of Dying***

"T.S. Eliot writes that *'We shall not cease from exploration, and at the end of all our exploring will be to arrive where we started, and know the place for the first time.'* Gifford and Sam Keen's book *Prodigal Father, Wayward Son* lays out in raw, intensely honest form, through a sharing of letters, the story of their reconciliation. To be a witness to their own 'knowing' that place of forgiveness, acceptance, and love gives hope that it is never too late to make up and (re)birth a parent/child relationship."

**—Lee Rush, trainer and consultant, International Institute for Restorative Practices and member, International Mankind Project**

"A very brave book about healing. It movingly portrays the very words and process of reconciliation between a father and a son: The courageous voicing and healing of old wounds and deep shame. Underneath that, they discover the deeper love that was always there, but thwarted. You can't read this book without wishing it could happen in your own family. Of course it can. May this book inspire healing and the rediscovery of love in our families, communities, and the world. We sure need it."

**—Glen Schneider, author of *Ten Breaths to Happiness***

"In their simply yet elegantly told story, the Keens have laid bare the inevitable struggles of fathers and sons. It is a book rich with compelling and engaging anecdotes that reveal male foolishness, abuses of power, and repeated rejections halted only by a painfully awkward — but inspiring and insightful — pursuit of reconciliation."

**—Bill Jersey, film producer/Peabody Award winner**

# PRODIGAL FATHER

## Wayward Son

### A ROADMAP TO RECONCILIATION

SAM KEEN AND GIFFORD KEEN

**DIVINE**
ARTS

Published by DIVINE ARTS
DivineArtsMedia.com

An imprint of Michael Wiese Productions
12400 Ventura Blvd. #1111
Studio City, CA 91604
(818) 379-8799, (818) 986-3408 (Fax)
www.mwp.com

Cover design by Johnny Ink. johnnyink.com
Copyediting by Ross Plotkin
Book design by Debbie Berne

Printed by McNaughton & Gunn, Inc.
Saline, Michigan
Manufactured in the United States
of America

Keen, Sam.
Prodigal Father, Wayward Son: A Roadmap to
Reconciliation / Sam Keen and Gifford Keen.
      pages cm. —
1. Keen, Sam. 2. Keen, Gifford, 1960– 3. Fathers and
sons. 4. Interpersonal conflict. 5. Reconciliation. I. Keen,
Gifford, 1960- II. Title.

HQ755.85.K443 2015
306.874'2--dc23

2014030967

Printed on recycled paper

# Contents

## PART III
## RITES OF PASSAGE

## PART IV
## HOMECOMING

# An Invitation to a Journey

This book is composed primarily of a series of stories told by a father and son to each other. Many of them are very personal and describe some of our most painful and tender memories. They are the pivotal stories that shaped our relationship and informed our characters as fathers, sons, and men.

But it is not only an account of how we rediscovered each other; it also illustrates a powerful process that can help other fathers and sons reconcile.

Some fathers and sons have horrific histories of alcoholism or abuse. But far more often, the wounds between fathers and sons are subtler. Ours is an all-too-common account of an absent father, alienated from his family by career and divorce, and a neglected, resentful son still longing for the affection of his father long after reaching manhood.

For decades we didn't get along. We loved each other, but we didn't like each other. Most of the time, it wasn't much fun to be together. Simple conversations could escalate into angry arguments in seconds. We couldn't get past our old wounds and forgive each other — no matter how much we wanted to or how hard we tried. With Sam approaching eighty and Gifford past fifty with a family of his own, it began to seem unlikely that we would ever make peace.

Then, two years ago, driven by a particularly bitter fight, we took a chance and began to exchange a series of letters in which we explored the roots of our conflicts. We journeyed back in time and space, searching out long-forgotten, often painful memories, and soon discovered that each of us had a small handful of anecdotes that came up over and over and seemed emotionally charged out of proportion to their content.

We began asking our male friends for stories about their fathers, and were amazed to find this phenomenon was universal. The stories themselves differed wildly — some were more positive and pleasant, others, far more horrifying than anything we'd experienced. But in every case, each man's relationship to his father was, in a fundamental way, defined by no more than half a dozen stories.

When we took the time to write our handful of stories and share them with each other, it became shockingly clear that those memories, so strongly preserved for so many years, had become the lenses through which we unconsciously interpreted all of our interactions. We realized these few stories were the root cause of the animosities we were unable to overcome.

Once these myths were examined in the light of day, they began to lose their power. It was as if a dam in the river of remembrance had broken. The grey impressions of the past were swept away, and hundreds of new memories that had long been repressed came tumbling forward, spilling into our minds, and filling our relationship with light, color, and compassion.

Soon the process took on a life of its own, and decades of rancid resentment melted away. Our conversations flowed with the ease, respect, and affection that we had always sensed should be ours. Everything changed. Not to say it was always easy — we still fought and continue to fight; at times, it required courage and patience to face stories that were unkind and painful. But the new memories that emerged helped us heal.

This book is a chronicle of our journey and the unexpected fruit it bore. It is a testimony to the power of personal mythology and the healing potential of storytelling. But we encourage readers to remember that, however personal our stories may be, they are also an invitation to a journey. They demonstrate a method by which fathers and sons can recognize the roots of their basic enmities, unravel ingrained assumptions, and heal longstanding wounds.

Use this book as a map to explore those key memories and stories that define your relationships. Write them down. Tell them to each other. See what happens. Perhaps the results will be as remarkable for you as they were for us.

# Prologue

There must always be a struggle between a father and son,
while one aims at power and the other at independence.

— Samuel Johnson

**SAM:** It should have been a moment for celebration.

It was one of those crystalline days with azure skies and a brisk wind blowing through the aspens that make people fall in love with Santa Fe. We had spent the best part of a weekend hiking the trails above town, struggling to resolve quarrelsome issues and ancient resentments that had haunted our relationship since you were a small son and I a fearsome father.

**GIF:** At the time, to all outward appearances, you and I were the best of friends. I was finally making good: married, kids, retired at forty from a successful high-tech career. We spoke on the phone every week, got together on holidays. You bragged about me to your friends.

But on another level, we had been stuck for many years in a strange purgatory. Underneath the surface camaraderie, on some half-unconscious plane, we were still continuing the guerrilla warfare that had been our shared burden since I was a child. Subtly, without intention, I'd kept the narrative that you were a rotten father alive. You countered with a competing, unarticulated narrative that, despite your long-ago shortcomings as a father, our current difficulties all stemmed from my inability to grow up, to let go of the past, to be a Man.

In short, although we had built your house together, gone camping and hiking, and shared hundreds of hours of conversation, we were still stuck in the destructive, power-based relational patterns established when I was a boy.

During the last three days, I had talked frankly to you about the understated ways you were still putting me down, constantly assuring yourself of your position as alpha male in our little pack. We discussed how our chronic, low-level discomfort was caused by old destructive patterns still being played out in our current interactions.

You told me how painful it was that I continued to bring up the divorce and those awful years. I spoke of my frustration with your ambivalence — how at times you were supportive, then at others so carelessly demeaning.

For the first time in ten years, we were making real progress on a previously intractable problem. Both of us were filled with the hope that we would finally be able to shed our skins and settle into that easy, elusive friendship we'd always felt was possible but that had somehow escaped us, floating tantalizingly just beyond our grasp.

**SAM:** I was due to return home that afternoon, so we decided to treat ourselves to breakfast at Café Pasqual's. After huevos rancheros and café latte, we were walking down Water Street. I was congratulating myself on a weekend of civil conversation during which we had managed to talk productively about old injuries resulting from my divorce and leaving home.

**GIF:** And then it happened.

"So," you asked, "what are you going to do now that you're not working?" It was casually said, but there was a nasty gleam in your eye, a critical tone in your voice.

This seemingly innocent comment struck deep. It was as if the only effect of all our recent conversation had been to expose my most vulnerable wounds to your disparagement. You might as well have said, "What kind of a worthless man sits around the house meditating and taking care of the kids? It doesn't matter how much money you have, you'll never be a Real Man — like me — until you do something worthwhile in the world."

"You've been feeding me this same crap since I was a kid," I said. "I quit my job because I hated it, and unlike you, I wanted to spend time with my children."

So easily, so smoothly, without thought or volition, I fell back into those old, familiar dance steps. *You were always inadequate, a lousy father; you abandoned me, and I'll never forgive you* was my unspoken message.

"I thought you weren't going to do this anymore," you replied angrily. "I've paid for my mistakes, and it's about time you realized it. So I'm telling you for the last time: Just knock this shit off."

Two to tango. What you really meant was: *Quit whining. The only problem here is that you're too weak to get over things that happened thirty years ago. And besides, I'm a man and you're just a boy. I've been kicking your ass since the day you were born, and I'll keep doing it till the day I die.*

**SAM:** Suddenly, without warning, you were possessed by a fit of blind rage. You stepped close, started poking me in the chest, and screamed in my face. "All that crap you did to me as a child is still going on. You're still bullying me." I was baffled by the attack. It seemed to come out of no-where, just when I thought we had reached a new level of understanding and forgiveness.

When I registered the charges that were being hurled at me, and the rage behind them, my frustration overflowed its banks, and I also began to shout.

"I have told you a hundred times how sorry I am for the pain I caused you by abandoning the family thirty years ago, but I thought we agreed that we weren't going to do this dance anymore. No more guilt trips."

**GIF:** I was overcome by white-hot wrath.

"Fuck you," I shouted. "Ever since I could remember, you've been pushing me around, cutting me down, intimidating me with your anger, browbeating me with you moronic Calvinistic values. And you're still doing it. Right now."

By this time we had stopped on the sidewalk and were facing each other; the tourists were starting to stare — but I didn't give a damn. I stepped up close and poked you hard in the chest, my face inches from yours, screaming at the top of my lungs.

"So listen up, you bombastic prick: I've spent my whole life terrified of your disapproval, trying to live up to your impossible standards, and I'm fed up with it. I don't give a damn if we end up best friends or if we never speak again, but I will not stand for this condescending bullshit ever again. Not one more time. It ends. Now!"

**SAM:** After a couple more violent interchanges, you started to walk away. Then you turned and stood firmly in the middle of Water Street. In a voice that drew a line in the sand, you shouted, "You're never going to push me around again. Never!" With that, you walked away, leaving me on the sidewalk — stunned.

**GIF:** A huge wave of relief washed over me. I didn't know what it would mean, but one way or another, it was over. We stared at each other in silence for a long moment, and then I turned and walked away, leaving you to your rental car and the long drive to the airport.

**SAM:** I made my way back to my car in a state of confusion and sat for an hour. Anger was gradually supplanted by profound grief. I drove aimlessly for an hour before I went to the café where we had agreed to meet to say goodbye before I was to catch my plane. I waited. I waited longer. After an endless time, I left town, engulfed in a cloud of despair. It seemed we would never exorcise the ghosts that haunted us and kept us from the intimacy we both wanted.

Thunderheads, harbingers of a coming storm, were gathering on the peaks of the Sangre de Cristo Mountains, rapidly obscuring the azure sky. As I drove south, I wondered if you would ever speak to me again. After trying and failing so many times to dissolve the lingering hostility that kept us apart, had we finally reached a dead end, a rupture that couldn't be healed?

How had we come to this?

Had I lost my son?

# PART I
# OFT-TOLD MYTHS

Nothing shapes our lives so much as the stories
we habitually tell and those we ignore.

– chapter 1 –

# Storytelling and Identity

I asked myself, "What myth are you living?" and found that I did not know.
So I took it upon myself to get to know "my" myth . . . I simply had to
know what unconscious or preconscious myth was forming me.

— C. G. Jung

**SAM:** After the fight at Pasqual's, it became clear we had come to a dead end. We were caught in a whirlpool of what Freud called "the repetition compulsion." We told the same stale, hurtful stories over and over, each repetition making it more difficult to see each other anew. It was obvious that no simple process of talking it through, minor tinkering, or psychotherapy would heal our relationship.

We needed to try something radically different. First, we had to deconstruct the oft-told myths that were keeping us in conflict; and second, we needed to tell the untold stories — the narratives of the lives we had created for ourselves, but had not shared with each other.

This amounted to a new understanding and practice of initiation.

Once upon a time, in tribal cultures, boys were formally initiated into manhood by elders who stole them from their parents, sequestered them, and taught them the official myths and rituals of their tribe or clan. These involved rites of passage in which boys were subjected to fearful ordeals — circumcision, long fasts, vision quests, scarification, walkabouts, killing an enemy — that were necessary to become a man.

Nowadays, we have only pale reflections of such tribal rituals — joining the Army, earning a driver's license, getting drunk in a bar upon turning twenty-one. But a strictly secular indoctrination lacks spiritual depth. The corporate, national, military, and consumer ideologies of our culture are fundamentally vacant and unsatisfying.

To create a meaningful initiation process, we must question the narratives that have become the unconscious foundations of our identities. Only then can we draw the venom from the oft-told myths and begin to understand the real origins of our conflict. We must go back to the beginning — peel back the veneer of the primal myths we have so often told to reveal the real stories they have occulted. Only then can we begin to understand the way our shared history and shared conflict have shaped our relationship.

This is an ambitious project, but it is still not enough. In addition to revisiting our shared stories, we need also to tell each other what we have *not* shared. This is a peculiarly modern problem. In the olden days, the elders knew the stories of the sons — because they lived together. But you and I spent all too little time together when you were young, and once you were grown, we lived far apart. So you have accumulated a vast storehouse of experience about which I know nothing.

What stories do I need to hear to understand how you became the man you are?

And what stories do I need to tell you so we can understand how life has defined our practice of manhood, and turned us into the fathers and sons we have become?

# chapter 2

# Abraham, Isaac, and the Egg

In the little world in which children have their existence . . .
there is nothing so finely perceived and so finely felt as injustice.

— Charles Dickens

**GIF:** Somehow, at a very early age, I became confused about the exact nature of the relationship between you and God.

My earliest memories are of a two-story redbrick house perched on a corner lot on a sleepy tree-lined street in Louisville, Kentucky, where we lived from the time I was two until I was eight. Mom stayed home with the kids while you spent your days teaching at the Presbyterian Seminary. Unsurprisingly, given your profession, religion was big in the Keen household: Bible stories, Sunday school, church every Sunday.

At the time, I was most familiar with the Old Testament, and I doubt I ever went so far as to think you actually *were* God. But it did seem to my young mind that you and God were much better acquainted with each other than I was with either one of you. Adding to my confusion was the apparently large number of character traits you had in common with Him.

First off, you were large and powerful with a huge voice. Omnipotent and omniscient. A stern and judgmental taskmaster, you were commonly absent, and unaccountably uninterested in my travails — much as God often seemed unconcerned with the plight of the Hebrews. Like God, you would descend at irregular intervals, sometimes lighting up the whole house with laughter and affection. When I nestled in your shoulder on Thursday nights to watch *The Rifleman* on TV, or sat in your lap while you told stories of fire fairies, I felt safe and warm, protected by your love. But at other times, your anger shook our home to the fundaments, leaving me sure I would be transformed into a pillar of salt.

I never knew which face you would show, beneficent or wrathful. And I could never determine any rhyme or reason to these moods — you were simply a force of nature. But as children do, I assumed *I* was responsible for your fits of temper.

In the end, although I didn't quite think you a deity, I did come to the conclusion that you were more like God than I was like you. This did not, unfortunately, result in the kind of respect or adoration I know you would have liked. Quite the opposite, as I became deeply troubled by Christianity at an early age.

Mom used to read to me almost every morning before school from a big picture book of Bible stories for kids. Normally it was a happy moment in the day; I would sit in her lap and enjoy her attention. But one morning, when I was five, she chose the story of Abraham and Isaac. Before we were halfway through, I was asking questions like, "What's a burnt offering?" and "What does God mean by 'sacrifice'?" I don't know whether she was unsettled or not, but she pressed on, and there on the last page was a horrifying drawing of little Isaac, bound and helpless, lying on a pile of wood. Abraham had this huge knife about two inches from poor little Isaac's throat, and it was obvious that the glowing angel staying Abraham's hand hadn't intervened until the last second.

In the picture, it looked like Abraham was fighting the angel.

I remember my head spinning all day at school. This was deeply screwed up — I mean, what about you? Would you slit my throat and burn me to a crisp if God told you to? In this context, the perception that you were on better terms with God than with me wasn't exactly reassuring. And what if the angel was late? Or God had forgotten to send him? And what kind of God would do something so obviously wrong?

I tried to forget about it, but the lingering suspicion that you would sacrifice my life to God's whim made a lasting impression, and I made a serious mental note to avoid taking long walks with you.

As it turns out, I was right to be suspicious. Less than six years later you did sacrifice me, and the rest of the family, on the altar of your quest for personal freedom. But I'm getting ahead of myself.

I remember the event that finally catalyzed the differentiation in my mind between you and God. It was a traumatic experience that at some level set us against each other and would haunt our relationship for decades to come.

This was the incident of "The Egg."

In the summer of 1966, when I was six, you bought a used VW van, removed the backseat, and replaced it with a wooden platform topped with a mattress — then packed up the family and headed out for a cross-country driving trip. There were no seatbelt laws in those days so as we drove from place to place, my sister and I frolicked on the double bed in the back of the van, playing games of our own devising. I periodically retired to the rectangular bin above the engine to sleep or read.

One early afternoon, somewhere in Middle America where it was flat, hot, and forested with large, deciduous trees, we stopped for lunch. Imagine the scene: the shiny VW van sitting in a field a hundred yards from a busy freeway, a checkered blanket stretched in the shade of a nearby tree with the remnants of our picnic lunch deserted along its margins. We were resting off the food, avoiding the moment when we would get back in the car. Mom had wandered off into the nearby woods in search of momentary privacy.

And then you called me. "Son, come over here this instant."

Your voice was low and dangerous, laced with ominous undertones, and I was already afraid by the time I came to where you were standing.

"What's this?"

You were pointing to the ground. And then I saw it: The Egg, an otherwise insignificant hardboiled egg, peeled and partially eaten, then rejected and inadequately concealed, abandoned with radioactive disregard behind the back wheel of the van.

"Why did you throw your egg in the dirt? You know we don't waste food."

"It's not mine. I ate my egg."

"Don't lie."

"I'm not," I pleaded, lower lip quivering. "Mom saw me eat it."

You lost it. Before I knew it, you were standing over me screaming at the top of your lungs, fists clenched, face red, the tendons in your neck stretched tight, like steel cords — as if you were channeling the very wrath of God.

Then you forced me to eat the egg. By the time I lifted it from the ground, it was covered with dirt. Twigs clung to the gummy surface. There were ants crawling on the partially masticated, pale yellow yolk. And you wouldn't even let me clean it off. It was a lesson. Children were starving in India. I would never be a Man if I didn't learn to tell the truth and own up to my mistakes.

I ate that damn egg. Dirt, sticks, ants, and all. All the while sobbing so hard I was afraid I would puke, begging you to relent, or at least to wait till Mom came back from taking a piss and ask her.

A few minutes after the deed was done, Mom returned to find me in tears, you in a rage, and my poor sister, Lael, cowering by the corner of the van.

"Gifford ate his egg," she told you. "It must be Lael's."

There was a note of admonition in her voice.

Fury thwarted, you turned on Mom. "Well, where the hell were you?"

"I was trying to squat somewhere the passing cars couldn't see up my pussy," she shouted. Mom almost never spoke back to you, especially in front of the kids, and I remember it well because it was the first time I'd ever heard the word "pussy."

After a tense silence, you turned away.

I thought then that you would admit your mistake and try to make amends, or at least that you would smite my sister, the true perpetrator of the heinous deed. But all you did was mumble something vaguely accusatory in her direction; then we got back in the van and drove away.

You never even said you were sorry.

For years the incident of the Egg loomed large in my psyche as a story of injustice. Not only was I falsely accused and received punishment disproportionate to the crime, but when the true culprit was uncovered, she was let off with nothing more than a weak reprimand. (It took a long time to realize that of all of us, this incident was probably the most traumatic for her — but that's another story.)

It wasn't until I had children of my own that I asked a much more obvious question: Why were you flying into a murderous rage, screaming at a six-year-old, humiliating him, making him eat dirt and ants — all over a five-cent egg?

Why were you so often angry with me when I was young?

# chapter 3

# Mother, Jesus, and Me

There is nothing that binds us so firmly as the chains we have broken.

— Howard Thurman

**SAM:** Your portrait of me as often angry and critical when you were young is true to my memory. But most of my anger wasn't caused by or even fundamentally directed toward you. You were a victim of collateral damage from an uncivil war that raged inside me for many years, the roots of which were entangled in both my ambivalent relationship with my mother's fundamentalist Christianity and my father's sexual taboos.

When I was a boy, Christianity was such an engulfing phenomenon as to be nearly invisible. I don't remember a time when I was not being indoctrinated body, mind, and spirit by the teachings of the Bible and the practices of the Presbyterian Church. Prayer and praise punctuated my days and weeks. Meals were prefaced with grace and occasionally with readings from Scripture. Before bed we said prayers, asked Jesus to come into our hearts, and implored God to forgive our sins. I was always fearful I had not repented sincerely enough and that my unconfessed (and, therefore, unforgiven) sins would condemn me to hell.

Sunday began with Sunday school and transitioned into the full adult eleven o'clock service. Having survived the morning, we repaired to the ritual dinner of consecrated roast beef, mashed potatoes, and gravy. This was followed by a dull afternoon in which we were supposed to "keep the Sabbath holy." Needless to say, dancing, cards, and movies were out of the question even on normal days, as was any word from *gosh* to *golly* that could be considered taking the Lord's name in vain. To this list of prohibited activities was added playing such boisterous games as Red Rover and Capture the Flag. To cap off the day, on many Sabbath evenings we were expected to go to Christian Endeavor for budding preteens, and afterward, evening church service. Do the math — four times every Sunday.

The high (or low) point of my "voluntary" acceptance of orthodox Christianity came one Sunday afternoon when I was a precocious eleven-year-old meeting in a dark, oak-paneled room with a dozen black-clad Presbyterian elders to determine if I was mature enough to join the church as an adult on confession of faith. It was highly unusual for a preadolescent to seek full membership, but my mother and grandmother, who were pillars of the church, promoted my candidacy. (Like Jesus) I answered the elders so well that I was congratulated for my mature understanding of the faith, then delivered to my proud mother and grandmother, who had been waiting with every assurance that I would pass the exam with glory to spare. Everyone was happy. It was a big deal.

But the worm was in the apple. It was only a matter of days before my halo faded, and I became intensely anxious. I had more doubt than faith. The idea that God would save only those who believed in Jesus seemed immoral, as did the mind-bending notion that we have free will but are predestined for salvation or damnation. No matter how I tried to believe in Him, I couldn't, and therefore I was forced to accept the conclusion that death, not eternal life, was my destiny.

The need to believe what I couldn't understand created conflict in my mind and a knot in my stomach. Each day I climbed into the treehouse that was my private sanctuary, read a chapter of the New Testament, and prayed I would be given true faith, graced with a personal relationship with my Lord and Savior, and spared both death and hell. But the more earnestly I sought faith, the stronger my doubts grew. This double bind left me with an abiding sense of failure.

As a Christian, I was required not only to believe the doctrines "once and for all delivered to the saints," but also to behave in a charitable and pacific manner, especially toward my enemies. Turn the other cheek. Practice humility. I made every effort to be a good boy, to repress my anger, and to avoid situations in which I might be forced to fight. I made an (unconscious) bargain: I would be a good Christian, imitate Jesus, and in return I would earn the approval of my mother and grandmother. As a result of agreeing to this Hobson's choice, I became critical of myself and, by association, of you too. I attacked myself for failing to be as gentle as Jesus, but at the same time I feared I was too gentle: a wimp, a sissy.

You asked if I was living a lie. The answer is both yes and no. On the one hand, I had a strong belief in the God who was the creator of birds, streams, clouds, the entire natural world I loved so much. But by the time you arrived in my life, I was in full rebellion against the fundamentalist myths I had been conditioned to believe.

To complicate matters, your mother, Heather (who had previously been a free spirit), admired my mother's religious certainty and converted to Christianity. Just as I thought I was escaping fundamentalism, it invaded the sanctuary of my marriage. When she insisted we attend church and that you go to Sunday school and learn your Bible stories, I feared you would be indoctrinated as I had been.

When I look back on these strange scenes from my childhood, I understand that I tried to believe the unbelievable because Mother needed me to. I conformed outwardly, but inwardly lived with constant anxiety. The more I struggled against the chains that bound me, the more I suffered from the painful knowledge that I was rejecting what Mother considered the greatest gift she could give me — True Religion. For her, belief in the fundamentals of Christianity was not a matter of life or death. It was far more important, a matter of eternal salvation or damnation.

Paradoxically, it was her passionate orthodoxy, abundant love, and unwavering commitment that created intellectual and emotional demands I could not fulfill, which in turn became twisted sources of my neurotic, idealized self-image, my betrayal of my essential self, and my subsequent anger that spilled over onto you.

How strangely we are wounded by those who love us most.

She tried to make me into her image of a Christian.

I tried to make you into my image of a man.

– chapter 4 –

# Men Don't Cry

I cannot think of any need in childhood as strong
as the need for a father's protection.

— Sigmund Freud

**GIF:** When I was very young, I used to sleep in a crib downstairs in the Kentucky house in a small alcove off the kitchen that was later destined to become the breakfast nook. When I got a little older, maybe four or five, I graduated to a room of my own. At the time, it seemed a big step into the adult world, and I was proud of my new status — but it was scary as well.

To a boy, that old house was gigantic, and my new upstairs room seemed far, far from the kitchen, the living room, and most importantly, the bedroom where you and Mom slept. The distances, which would now be but a few steps, at the time seemed continental. The two flights of stairs, doglegged around a wide landing, were mountain ranges for me to explore. The narrow room that ran the length of the second story was my own private country, a vast expanse where adults rarely came and my sister and I could rule as we saw fit.

Up the steep stairs, across that open space, tucked under the eaves, was my new room. It was cozy and light with two windows overlooking the roof of a long, covered porch. A small bed sat in one corner, and across from it loomed a big closet with an ill-fitting door that had an eerie habit of drifting open without provocation.

And in the back of the closet was a three-foot-square hole in the drywall.

I don't know if the builders just never finished it or if it had been left on purpose to provide access. Whatever the case, when I stood in the dimly lit closet and pushed aside the clothes, I could peer into the hole and see way, way back into a dark, mysterious space that ran under the edge of the sloping roof, far out of sight in either direction. There was no real floor, only bare wooden joists with insulation between. It was dusty, dark, and creepy. Who knew where it went or what might live there?

On more than one occasion, you told me never, never, never to venture into the hole. It was dangerous, and I would "fall through." Not having a clear concept of architecture, I didn't realize that the living room lay beneath the eaves, and so I had no idea of where I would end up if I did fall through — leaving me with the suspicion that if I were foolish enough to venture into this dark, forbidden space, I would surely slip between the rafters, plunge into unknown, perilous depths filled with hellfire and damnation, and never be seen again.

Despite the fact that I was an adventurous boy, I had no desire to crawl into the hole, and over time I developed an aversion to even entering the closet.

Then one night, probably a year after moving upstairs, I had a dream: a horrible nightmare.

I was in my room with a friend from across the street. We were playing with Legos, immersed in our own world, far from the prying eyes of adults, when suddenly the closet door opened. A man came out. An ogre. And although he looked fairly normal (vaguely reminiscent of my maternal grandfather, actually), we knew right away that he was malign, unnatural, and not human. He asked what we were doing, and when I replied — something about how time passed differently for children than adults — he grabbed my friend by the shirt, lifted him into the air, and began to beat his face with a gigantic, knotty fist.

I awoke shaking, sure the ogre was standing still and silent in the dark at the foot of the bed. I knew he was there. Waiting, watching. As soon as I moved or made a sound, he would pounce and do . . . I didn't know what.

I lay there for the longest time, afraid to breathe, afraid to move. It was unbearable. Finally, not knowing what else to do, I threw back the covers, leapt from the bed, and ran, sure I felt his hot breath on my neck, expecting at any moment to be caught from behind. Out of my room, across the playroom, down the stairs, and out into the long, dark hallway that led to your bedroom.

When I got there, the door was closed. I was expressly forbidden to enter your bedroom uninvited, so I knocked. No response. I knocked louder and louder, banging on the wooden door with my little fists until at last you answered.

"What is it?" Your voice, filtered through the closed door, sounded none too pleased.

"There's an ogre in my room."

"No, there's not." A long pause. Then, "It's just a bad dream."

"No, he's there. Really."

"Go back to bed. We'll talk about it in the morning."

"He'll eat me."

"It's a just a dream," you repeated. "There's nothing there."

"Come and see."

"Don't be a coward." Your voice took on a dangerous, displeased edge. "Now let your mother and me sleep."

"Please, can't I come in? Just for a minute."

"I said no, and I mean no, and that's that. Now be a man and go get yourself back in bed."

This formulation, "Be a man," was all too familiar, and I knew from hard experience that I had reached the end of the line. Any further pleas or attempts to reason would only enrage you. You were not going to let me into your bedroom. You were not going to take me back to bed. I was on my own.

I sat down then on the cool hardwood floor outside your room, put my back against the wall, and wept.

Silently.

Afraid you would hear me.

Because I knew men weren't supposed to cry.

I stayed there for a long time, frightened out of my wits. But finally, after what seemed like hours, I realized that there was nothing else to do but go back to bed. There was nowhere else to go. I was cold. The floor was hard.

I don't think I have ever been as terrified since as I was then. That trip back along the dark hallway, up the stairs, and across the big playroom, knowing what was waiting for me when I arrived, was perhaps the hardest thing I've done in my life. I stopped outside my room, still too afraid to enter, sure the ogre was there, crouched at the foot of my bed or lurking just inside the hole in the closet; then, finally, I screwed my courage, dashed across the room, jumped into bed, and pulled the covers over my head.

It was three years before I slept with my back to that closet.

# chapter 5

# Dark and Anxious Times

An angry father is most cruel towards himself.

— Publilius Syrus

**SAM:** On November 4, 1964, at the age of sixty-four, my father died. You were four; I was thirty-three. The ground shook, and the landscape of fear changed forever. Freud said the death of the father is the most significant event in a man's life. It was in mine. I returned from his funeral changed: sadder, softer, and needier. I know you felt my sadness, and during that time you would often crawl into my lap and comfort me.

For three years, I tried to hide my grief. Heather said that in those years she never saw my tears, but sometimes when I came home from a late-night walk she knew I had been weeping. I felt out of control and anxious during most of my waking hours. A dark undertow was pulling me toward death. Everything was disintegrating. My public and private lives were emotionally light years apart. I was teaching at the seminary, but Christianity was losing its hold on me. None of its promises were powerful enough to stand against the stark reality of my father's death.

My marriage was in trouble. I had promised Heather that I would spend more time with the family once I had gotten a fulltime job. I didn't. She was unhappy, so I decided I would send her to therapy. She returned from her first session with Dr. M. with the disturbing news that he suspected I had "issues" with women, and suggested I come in for a session. I agreed. Why not? I was more than happy to help him solve her problem.

During my first therapy session, I explained to the dour doctor what Heather needed to do to get happy. He countered with the disturbing pronouncement that at least half the problems in the marriage were mine, and I might want to work on some of my "issues," like my anger at Heather, my mother, and my distrust of women in general.

I was outraged. How dare this shrink accuse me of harboring such vile feelings? I was teaching a course in the seminary about the varieties of love, and this bastard was suggesting I was filled with anger. The more I thought about it, the more furious I became.

My personal apocalypse occurred that afternoon as I was walking home across the park. Quite suddenly, my resistance melted; and, in a single gulp, I swallowed the bitter draught the grim doctor had prepared for me. Yes, goddamn it, yes! I was furious at Heather. And my mother. Women in general and Mother in particular were insatiable, impossible to please.

More than that, I was prey to completely irrational attacks of random anger. I was always cursing someone or something under my breath: an idiot driving too fast or too slow; some boring colleague; endless faculty meetings; dull students and stupid fundamentalists who refused to think; the goddamned war in Vietnam. By the time I reached the far side of the park, the happy, energetic self I had considered myself to be evaporated before the monster. I walked home, lost in a wilderness with the painful knowledge that I had to begin a journey of self-discovery.

Shortly after my descent into the nether kingdom, Dr. M. recommended we take a six-week marriage sabbatical during which we would try to un-tangle the sources of our conflict. Despite concerns about how Heather would manage in my absence, I agreed. (As it turned out, without my au-thoritarian presence in the house, the atmosphere was lighter. Mom taught you and Lael how to catapult peas off spoons at the dinner table, and she rose splendidly to the challenge of being a single parent.)

By midsummer I traveled to Princeton and rented an apartment on the edge of campus. On the first night, as darkness came on, I began to feel I had made a terrible mistake. I'd never been alone for more than a night or two and had not acquired the skills that made solitude rich, or even bearable. I had no sooner closed the door of my apartment than I felt lonesome and anxious. I cooked dinner, brewed tea, and forced myself to read *Sons and Lovers*. Mercifully, sleep arrived around page 100.

Morning came and stretched before me like an empty canvas. By midafternoon the anxiety was intolerable. I felt like a victim of a disease without a name. So I went to the library to see if I could find anything that would speak to my condition. Trusting in luck, I pulled book after book off the shelf, browsed for a moment, and waited for a relevant sentence to jump off the page. For hours I wallowed in Freud, Jung, and Adler without finding any soul food.

I was about to abandon my hit-or-miss method when Karen Horney's *Neurosis and Human Growth* jumped into my hand, and lightning struck. I sat and read, transfixed by finding my condition described on every page. That evening, after purchasing a copy of the book, I began to mark passages in red, and soon I could make out the topography of my troubled psyche.

For the first time I had a name for my condition: neurosis.

According to Horney, neurosis is a character disorder in which a person suffers from a split between the real and idealized selves, which produces a continual oscillation between feelings of superiority and inferiority. At one moment, the neurotic has a glorified, omnipotent self-image. At the next, he falls into feelings of impotence and self-hatred. When he isn't judging others for stupidity or cowardice, he turns his withering gaze on himself. Neurotic individuals inevitably fail to live up to their image of their idealized self. They consequently suffer continual anxiety and feel there is a flaw inside that must, but cannot, be corrected.

I was both appalled and heartened by these discoveries. For the first time, I had a map that showed me the logic of my emotional ups and downs. I began to notice that when I was in the grip of feelings of superiority, I became judgmental of everyone around me, but especially of you.

At the time, it seemed clear that you were far from perfect, and it was my responsibility to instruct you. But somehow it didn't occur to me that my efforts to improve you were, in fact, intimidating and cruel. Nor did

I notice that when I judged you, I soon began to lacerate myself and fall prey to feelings of inferiority. I think the brunt of my neuroses fell on you because, as my son, I most identified with you. So I treated you as I treated myself. I was alternately kind and neglectful. Sometimes we would play and wrestle on the bed, or I would bury myself in the newspaper when I came home from work and ignore you.

Oddly enough, all through this time I worried much more about you than your sister. Lael was an easy baby — affectionate, happy, and, for the most part, eager to please. She and I had little conflict, and I was kinder and gentler with her than with you. I did not feel I had any special wisdom about how girls were to become women, so I had a much more laissez-faire attitude about her upbringing. Having been a boy who became a man, I (erroneously) considered myself an expert on how a son — you — should become a Man — with a capital M.

I was so self-absorbed and distracted during those six difficult years in Kentucky that I did not realize the effect my neurosis was having on you.

# chapter 6

# Log and Posthole

The father who does not teach his son his duties is equally
guilty with the son who neglects them.

— Confucius

**GIF:** Work was always a bone of contention for us, and I realize now that
very early on we established unfortunate patterns that played out for many
years afterward — all the way up to that day at Pasqual's.

You set me impossible tasks as a boy that I couldn't hope to achieve,
and systematically ignored my accomplishments. Often, when I thought
I'd done something remarkable, you were indifferent. You praised deeds
I considered inconsequential, and punished me for things I didn't think
were wrong.

Nowhere is this juxtaposition more obvious than with two early memories I have of working in the backyard of our house in Kentucky.

The first occurred on a hot summer day when I was five. You set a log
on a ratty pair of X braces next to the side of the garage and challenged
me to chop through it. I remember you standing above me, legs braced,
swinging the ax in a long glittering arc, the edge biting into the log with a
loud *thunk*, the wood chips flying through the air. "Like that," you told me,
then stalked off.

I don't remember what enticement you offered, perhaps money or some
privilege, but to me the real reward was obvious: this was a test, an initiation. Success, I felt certain, would open the door to the mythical realm
of Manhood. I would finally attain the longed-for balm of your approval.

But I couldn't do it. In my memory, that log is three feet thick. The X
braces were waist-high, so I couldn't get a good swing. The ax was longer

than I was tall, and dull as a butter knife. I chopped and chopped until sweat ran down my back, my arms shook with fatigue, and blisters opened on my palms. In the end, all I had to show for my efforts was a narrow, V-shaped groove no more than six inches wide and a couple inches deep. It didn't go an eighth of the way through.

You were, to say the least, unimpressed. I was humiliated and positive I would never be a Real Man, at least not until I could chop through that damned log — which I figured I could never do.

The second event took place later that same summer when you decided to build a wooden fence in the backyard. I watched with fascination as you and a friend set posts, mixed concrete, and suspended small line-levels filled with a mysterious yellow liquid on nylon string stretched taut between the posts. The fence was more than half done before I asked if I could dig one of the postholes. But, certain the posthole digger was too heavy and I too small to make the attempt, you wouldn't even let me try.

It was late in the evening, the sun had set, the heat of the day was dwindling, and the long summer twilight had just begun when you went inside to wash up and read the paper before dinner. The posthole digger had been left lightly planted in the ground at the site of the next hole. So when you went into the house, I dug.

It is still a sweet memory of triumph. The air was cool, the gentle evening breeze caressing my skin as I lifted the posthole digger and dropped it into the ground again and again, working the handles, pulling the dark loam out of the hole, and releasing it onto an ever-growing pile. By the time Mom called me to dinner, it was almost full dark and the posthole was three feet deep.

You had to fill in a third of it the next day before setting the post.

It is almost impossible to reconcile my early recollections of you with the man I know today. Yet I have so many memories of you telling me, "You'll never be a man if you don't learn to work." You were always on me:

"Quit malingering. Don't be a jellybean. Throw yourself into the job." You seemed obsessed with turning me into a man, and it seemed like I always came up short of the mark. And not just a little.

At some point — probably before I was six — I accepted it. I knew, with the kind of clarity that only comes to small children, that I fundamentally lacked the basic stuff of manhood, that the manly virtues you so prized were simply not to be found within my narrow chest, and that no matter how hard I tried, I would never be anything but a disappointment to you.

So I gave up on you and stopped even trying to be a good son.

– chapter 7 –

# Sex and Taboo

The contradictory commands issuing from the Freudian superego say both
"thou shalt be like the father" and "thou shalt not be like the father."

— Norman O. Brown

**SAM:** In 1939, the year I turned seven, my family moved to the little town
of Boaz, Alabama, home to five hundred souls who were on intimate terms
with poverty. Dad had been offered his first fulltime position teaching
choral music at Snead Junior College. We lived in a rambling house with a
potbelly stove for heat and a wood-burning range for cooking. Our nearest neighbors were a pair of sisters who'd had a falling-out a generation
earlier; they had stopped talking to each other, had their house sawed in
half, boarded up, and the halves moved thirty feet apart. We raised a large
garden and had a prolific pecan tree. Two dogs, a cat, and twenty Rhode
Island Red chickens (to whom Dad sang each afternoon, claiming it made
them lay more eggs) completed the ménage.

To say Boaz was short on culture would be an understatement. At that
time, Sand Mountain County was reckoned to be the second poorest in
the United States. (Now it is a Mecca for outlet stores.) Even though the
country at large was on the recovering edge of the Depression, local farmers scratched a bare subsistence out of growing cotton and came to town
on Saturdays in mule-drawn wagons. In this context, Dad was the biggest
cultural event in town. In short order he recruited forty students (most of
whom had never traveled outside Alabama), gave them voice lessons, and
molded them into a tight choir. When it came time for their debut recital,
all were dressed in black-and-white outfits, and the local people filled every seat in the college auditorium. The image of Dad in his tux and tails

conducting that great choir remains etched in my heart. I believe that in that brief moment he responded fully to his vocation, and his accomplishment matched his dream.

The events that followed this triumph changed all of our lives. Even today what really happened, and what was only imagined, remains shrouded in the half-light of memory.

The crisis arrived like a tornado on an otherwise-ordinary summer afternoon. When my brother Lawrence and I emerged from the woods where we had been damming up the stream, Mother informed us that the next morning we would be moving back to Maryville, Tennessee, where my grandmother lived, and we should pack a small bag of our favorite toys. I chose my bird books, binoculars, and slingshot, and waited for whatever was coming next.

Just before dusk, the sheriff arrived, sat in a rocking chair on the porch with a shotgun resting on his lap, and began his vigil. We were confused because we knew him from an occasion when he had killed a rabid dog near our house, but there was no such obvious danger now. Dad and Mother brought him coffee and talked with him at length. We noticed men loitering on the street and more cars than usual cruising by, but when we asked what was happening, we were told that all would be explained the next day. The atmosphere of danger and drama only grew thicker when we were ordered to remain in the house and keep the doors locked. When morning came, we stuffed the car with all it would hold and turned the house key over to friends from the college who would pack our furniture for the movers.

The sheriff escorted us out of town, and we were on the road to a new life.

When we were well out of the county and had shaken off the dust of Boaz, Mother explained what had happened. She and Dad had befriended a young woman in the choir — Mary-Grace — who came from a family too dirt-poor to buy an outfit for the recital, and they had taken her shopping in a nearby town. She had written a flowery thank-you note that fell into the hands of her father, leading him to believe that she and Dad had been having an affair. The truth, Mother said, was that she had a crush on Dad, but there had been no affair. The irate father had begun to assemble his friends to go over to the Yankee Professor's house and . . . it was not clear what they intended, but the Sheriff knew loose talk could lead to violence, and he and my parents decided it would be best for all if we left town.

The story might have ended here, but some months after we fled Boaz, Mary-Grace appeared on the scene and, on occasion, babysat for us. Several years later Dad told us, in a voice heavy with barely suppressed rage, that Mary-Grace had fallen in love with a naval officer, gotten pregnant, had an illegal abortion, and died.

These were the only "facts" we were told, and the whole affair was blanketed in silence. It wasn't to be talked about!

After Mary-Grace's death, Dad frequently expressed violent disapproval of sex outside marriage. He would explode with righteous anger and proclaim, "I loathe people who mess around with sex when they aren't married." Although I was too young to fully understand the temptation against which I was being cautioned, my teenage mind feared invoking some terrible judgment were I to break the taboo.

Why did he become so violent in his prohibitions of extramarital sex? Was his vehemence a guilty reaction to a sexual indiscretion? Or righteous indignation for resisting an affair he passionately desired? Or an expression of profound grief for a young woman he loved, purely or otherwise?

We never knew. But whatever the case, after this event, Dad never regained his governing passion for music. Above all, he was a musician — a violinist and a choirmaster. He might have been great, but after the Boaz debacle, he gave up music and went into the business of selling nurses' uniforms. Outwardly, he made this sacrifice because he couldn't provide for our family on a choirmaster's salary; but there came a time, when his uniform business wound down, that he might have returned to his first love. And he didn't. I believe he lost his nerve and, as a result, lived with a sense of failure and sadness. He fulfilled all the promises he made to his children but broke the promise he made to himself.

By the early 1960s his health deteriorated, and he and Mother settled in the pristine town of Prescott, Arizona. They got a sun-drenched apartment and lived with a quiet sense of contentment. It was, Mother said, the happiest time of their marriage. He died at the age of sixty-four — far too early.

I loved him outrageously but could never shake the feeling that, in some measure, the asthma and emphysema that killed him were the result of contradictions within his spirit. Caught between the needs of his family and the pursuit of his vocation, he abandoned the source of his joy. After his death, I realized his lack of fulfillment haunted me, leaving me with a deep sadness that was both his and mine. And that sadness engendered an iron resolve never to abandon my passion, never to repeat his mistake.

Out of loyalty to his unfulfilled passion, I vowed I would never live in the shadow of his shadow.

# chapter 8

# Ghost Stories

An idea, like a ghost, must be spoken to a little before it will explain itself.

— Charles Dickens

**GIF:** It is startling to reread the stories of our early conflicts, to see them rendered in black and white, starkly printed on the page with no room for equivocation, no way to evade their poignancy or soften their sting. In one way, this handful of stories is as familiar to me as my own face in the mirror. They have been a part of me for so long, I had almost forgotten they were there. Riding my shoulder, whispering in my ear, their voices just below the threshold of perception, these haunting memories have exercised a profound effect upon our relationship.

Over the years, as my psyche evolved around them, these stories became strangely opaque. Like a collection of sealed boxes with a label on the front, each one stood whole — a simple, shorthand symbol for the whirlwind of complex emotional responses packed inside. Unopened, over-told, unexamined, I was unable to interpret them from any perspective but that of the child who had crammed those memories into boxes, slammed the lids, and turned the keys so many years ago.

But now, when I take them out, dust them off, and render them into writing, the stories seem very strange. So often polished with unconscious retelling, they have an overproduced, movielike quality as if they were made up or had happened to someone else. And in truth, hard as I try, I can barely recognize either you or myself as the actors in these spectral plays.

———

When we fought outside Pasqual's on that bright fall day over a decade ago, it felt as if, despite our best efforts, years of therapy, and hours of conversation, not one bloody thing had changed. Because at some fundamental level, nothing had. Even though as adults we had built your house together, supported each other through our respective divorces, and become in some ways close friends, in a very real sense I did not know you — nor did you know me. And these stories were the culprits.

They held us hostage, shackled us to a mythic past that perhaps had never even happened.

How could this be?

How do I know you?

How does any son know his father?

Once I was grown and gone from the house, the main way I knew you was through memories. Yet memories only remain vivid if they are taken out and refreshed from time to time, if we tell them to others or ourselves as stories. And somehow, through some dark alchemical process, the stories I have told here, along with a small handful of similar ones, became the distorted lens through which I knew you. And whatever our differences, I have always loved you, so these stories, no matter how painful, were powerful and precious. Yet reading them now, I see so clearly (I wonder how I could have ever missed it) that the people in these narratives are long gone, or maybe largely creations of our own imaginations.

And it is a bitter irony to realize that the phantom mythos to which I clung so tightly (precisely because I thought it was the essence of how I knew you) was the very thing that prevented us from seeing each other. The haunted past intruded on the present, standing between us, thwarting our most diligent attempts to achieve what we most wanted: to know one another.

The more I think about it, the odder it strikes me that so much of our relationship, even as adults, was so strongly influenced by such a small number of mythic stories. For me, these tales were like a scratch in an old vinyl record. They played over and over, the groove becoming deeper with each repetition, the needle never progressing to the next track. Like a bad habit, or an addiction, these few harsh images stood sentinel at the entry-way to memory and experience, restricting my responses to you to a very narrow range.

But why were these particular stories promoted to mythic proportions? This is perhaps the strangest, most perplexing question of all. It seems certain there were hundreds, if not thousands of other stories I could have chosen, some better, some probably worse. So why these? Was it brain chemistry, karma, some psychological choice I made as a small child?

Whatever the case, I cannot help but wonder what alternate histories we could construct from the vast storehouse of memory. What would our lives be like if we could view our memories like a movie, sort through them, and consciously choose the ones we wanted to promote to mythic status? How would that change the future?

How would it change the past?

# PART II
# SELDOM-TOLD STORIES

We create ourselves by choosing a handful of memories
from the vast archives of remembrance.

– chapter 9 –

# Portrait of My Father

I believe that what we become depends on what our fathers teach us at odd moments,
when they aren't trying to teach us. We are formed by little scraps of wisdom.

— Umberto Eco

**SAM:** In the last years, when you and I have tried to disentangle ourselves from our long history of conflict, I have come to realize that the stories about my father provide a distant mirror in which I can see multiple reflections — images of him, myself, you, and your son all mixed together.

Above all, my father was an anomaly, a bundle of contradictions — mostly happy. With the exception of his taboos surrounding extramarital sex, he was a Dionysian character, full of passion and spontaneity.

Maybe the best way to introduce him is by sharing a letter I received in 1986 from one of his students who remembered his influence on her a half-century earlier.

*Dear Sam Keen,*

*When I was a senior in high school there came into Knoxville's provincial midst a man — very much a pied piper — who charmed the musical sensibilities of most folks but at the same time repulsed their properness. In those days, the University of Tennessee had no School of Music. Then Pop Keen came.*

*Pop Keen was the first intensely serious, honest-with-the-edges-cut, instead of smooth-polite, openly emotional man-person I had ever seen. When he came to UT in 1937 to lead a music program, I joined his chorus. No matter that we were all untrained in music, he exacted his professional standards. He lectured. He paced. He cursed. And I was fascinated. A girlfriend of mine found his language offensive and dropped out. I recognized in his zeal and professionalism a new drumbeat I had never heard, much less marched to in Knoxville. In my freshman year, we sang Brahms'* Requiem. *It was a high moment — possibly the first epiphany in my young life.*

*J. Alvin Keen was something of an enigma to conservative East Tennesseans. Possibly so to his own family. Doubtless so to himself. I watched tears run down his cheeks at a Marian Anderson concert when she sang, "Were you there when they crucified my Lord?" I saw peace and satisfaction, almost awe, show on his face when our scratchy little chorus of voices rendered a particular section of music to his satisfaction. All of his restless energy he spent for such brief ecstatic moments. It seems to me now that life and its richness was always just beyond his grasp. I believe it is ever thus for the psyche which is creative. I learned valuable technique about choral singing for which I have always been grateful, but Pop Keen taught me many more valuable things: like a fresh point-of-view, a rugged authenticity, and the discovery that small-town evil and even small-town promise and fulfillment are less than absolute, and possibly even trivial. He didn't just open a new door for me, bless him; he was a whole new world. After some months of exposure to this Zorba, I decided I could (with guilt yet) read* Gone With the Wind *and slip off to Maryville to see Hedy Lamarr in* Ecstasy.

*I don't know what others thought of him. I don't believe he cared a lot. Only tenderness for his sensitive wife and family might have gnawed at his Dionysian heart, but his idiosyncrasies and handicaps distinguished him as the lovable tyrant he was. He added a dimension to my life that was both cacophonous and harmonious.*

*If you are anything like your dad, you must be pretty great.*

*Tout bien,*
*Barbara Rule Moorman*

The father I knew during my first decade of life — the music man — had a passion for music and for his family. Before marrying Mother (who accompanied him on the piano when he gave violin concerts when she was eleven and he twenty-one), he traveled on the Chautauqua circuit with the Royal Male Quartet. When the soprano absconded with the group's funds in Montana, the quartet suddenly became a trio, and he more or less settled down, married, and enrolled in the Westminster Choir School. After taking a master's degree at the University of Iowa, he moved to Knoxville, where he patched together a living teaching music and directing choirs at various churches and at the University of Tennessee.

Dad's best friend, Norval Martin, ran the university shop where he crafted whatever mechanical gadgets were needed by professors. With endless ingenuity, he created for my father a precursor of a high-fidelity sound system cobbled together with large speakers and the flywheel of a Packard that was so perfectly balanced, it would spin for twenty minutes after it had been turned off. Once installed in our house on the edge of the campus, the neighborhood was treated to Bach, Beethoven, and Brahms. Dad would crank the system to the max, cup one hand behind his ear, pace the floor, and sing along at the top of his rich, baritone voice. When Mother suggested he might turn down the volume so as not to disturb the neighbors, Dad reminded her that the fraternity house across the street showed no such consideration for us when they had parties on Friday nights. And certainly, he opined, it was better to broadcast Bach than bop! And there the discussion ended.

Once when we were on the Cherokee Indian Reservation in Eastern Tennessee, Dad bought Lawrence and me bows and arrows. He cautioned us not to play with them in the car. Unable to resist temptation, I threaded an arrow into my bow, then accidentally let fly. The arrow *zinged* with appalling force right past his ear and hit the windshield.

Startled, Dad reared back and raised his fist as if to hit me. But he didn't. It was one of the few times I ever saw him angry with anyone in the family. He told me later that when he saw the look of terror on my face, he was ashamed.

———

Dad radiated such a sense of unquestionable authority, it was inconceivable that any of his children (or choir members) would defy him. Never once did he resort to the kind of bullying tactics I used (unsuccessfully) with you. We all knew that underneath his stern exterior was inordinate love and a disposition toward mercy. He was constitutionally unable to stay angry with any of his children for more than a few minutes.

One Sunday morning, Lawrence and I were deposited on the front pew of the Westminster Presbyterian Church in Knoxville with the admonition to behave during service. Somewhere between the doxology and the pastoral prayer, our tolerance for sedentary piety evaporated, and we began sliding to opposite ends of the long, oak pew, then sliding back until we collided in the middle. Lost in what we considered normal play — in those days all boys were hyperactive — we didn't notice that Dad had descended from the choir loft and was approaching with deliberate speed. He grabbed each of us by an arm, half-carrying, half-dragging us down to the basement of the church into a dim room that contained a large furnace, an office, and a hangout for the very large, very black, very kind janitor — Leonard. Dad peeled off a dollar bill and told Leonard to take us to the drugstore and buy us ice cream.

Buy us ice cream? We could only imagine we were being fattened for the kill, given a taste of the sweet before bitter punishment was to fall on us. Church ended. Dad fetched us. We drove home waiting for our just desserts, but retribution never arrived. Nothing was ever said about the event.

We moved to Maryville in 1943, after leaving Boaz under a dark cloud. The mysterious doings at the Oak Ridge Laboratory were pumping money into the local economy, but none of it was funding the arts. Longhaired music wasn't going to defeat the Axis, so there were no jobs for choirmasters. With money in short supply, Dad took the only work available.

Granny, Katherine McMurray, taught home economics at the college, and during the Depression, she founded the College Maid Shop, which gave girls a way to work their way through college by sewing various kinds of uniforms. With the war, demand for uniforms for Navy and Army nurses burgeoned, and Dad became a traveling salesman, going from one military-hospital complex to another throughout the country. Typically, he would set up shop in the living room of the nurses' quarters and meet the nurses as they came off their shift. If they would fit into a standard size, he would take their orders; otherwise, he would measure them for tailor-made uniforms.

Gradually, his trips became longer and his time at home shorter. Occasionally, he would take one of us children along for company. But more often than not, we endured his long absences and waited for the candy man to return. Sometimes we would get a phone call, supposedly from some distant city, with the news that he would be home in a week. Ten minutes later he would pull into the driveway and begin disgorging a wealth of odd items and gifts he had picked up on his wanderings.

Once, when he was in the middle of Montana, he called and asked if we would like to have a stuffed buffalo head. Mother was eavesdropping on the conversation, and shook her head from side to side in a gesture that clearly meant, "No. Absolutely not!" Instead, he came home with a three-foot shell of a giant man-eating clam that still sits in my garden.

Dad had an outsized sense of wonder and ability to enjoy life. But he was far from perfect. He was a patriarch who expected to be obeyed without question, and the very force of his personality could be intimidating. It wasn't until I was (somewhat) reeducated by the woman's liberation movement that I realized I had inherited both his virtues and vices.

I mark the beginning of my expulsion from Eden as our 1943 departure from Maryville and subsequent relocation to Wilmington, Delaware. No one in the family wanted to leave Maryville, but we needed be near the manufacturer of the uniforms sold by the J. Alvin Keen Company. From the moment we drove through that bland city, with its culture shaped by the chemical giants, I knew I had been cast into exile. There were no woods within miles, nothing wild. I was enrolled in P.S. DuPont High School, and for five years felt out of place and depressed.

Wilmington was also a game-changer for Dad — a spiritual swamp, a bad dream, and a fall from grace in more ways than one. To begin with, the chemical plants on both sides of the Delaware River — DuPont, Atlas, and Hercules — and the oil refineries in Marcus Hook spewed noxious fumes into the air that escalated his asthma into full-scale emphysema; this so restricted his breathing that he could not remain in the city for more than a few weeks at a time.

Gradually, he became the superfluous head of the household, spending more and more time hustling a declining market for nurses' uniforms. While Mother handled the business — correspondence, packaging, shipping, and billing — he spent more time in the Southwest roaming around Indian reservations, searching for places he could breathe.

By nature, Dad was a wanderer given to impractical enthusiasms. Among other things, while traveling in the Southwest, he fell in love with Navajo rugs and jewelry and regularly returned with a couple thousand dollars' worth of goods — which he (reluctantly) sold to admirers just in time to cover the checks he had sprinkled around various trading posts (but had never bothered to add up). That, also, was Mother's job.

When Dad was at home he was restless; when he was traveling for business or staying in the desert climate of the West where he could breathe, he was lonely. This pattern of constant movement made him an outsider, never part of a community. Like him, I have never been quite at home.

# chapter 10

# The Keen Way

Every man has his folly, but the greatest folly of all . . . is not to have one.

— Nikos Kazantzakis

**GIF:** When I read these wonderful stories about your father, the gates of memory opened, and dozens of stories about you that I had completely forgotten came flooding into my mind. Even though I never really knew your father, seeing him through your eyes rekindled my memories of your verve and spontaneity — which I see so clearly in your memories of him.

Here are some of the things I remembered.

When I was a boy, you used to tell me, "There's the wrong way, the right way, and then there's the Keen Way." I didn't have to ask, not even the first time. It was obvious: the Keen Way was superior. Because we, the Keens, were doing it, whatever it was, it was even righter than the right way.

As a child and then later as a teenager, I often found your unconventional behavior mortifying. Apparently the Keen Way included changing your swimsuit in the parking lot at the beach in front of God and everybody. When chided, you would laugh and say, "If they've seen one before, it's nothing new, and if they haven't, it's about time they did."

You used to rummage through the neighbors' garbage, dig through dumpsters, and retrieve furniture, clothing, or household goods in various states of disrepair. And you didn't even try to hide it. Far from it! In fact, you loved to boast about your finds. Standing astride a massive trash pile, holding some prize above your head, you would call across the street in a booming voice to wherever we were cowering in embarrassment that some idiot (obviously not a Keen) had thrown out a perfectly good toaster.

You were famous for rescuing "road kill." This had nothing to do with dead animals (thank God), but rather with retrieving "useful" items from the side of the road. In the dog days of summer, you used to pack the family into the back of a green-and-white VW bus and take us on long trips to various semi-exotic locations. (If you live in the suburbs of Louisville, Kentucky, almost anywhere else seems exotic.)

At least once a trip, sometimes once a day, without warning, you would jam on the brakes and swerve precipitously to the side of the highway. Then, cackling in maniacal glee, with your head stuck out the open driver's-side door, you would back up along the shoulder at full speed, the engine whining, oblivious to the honking horns and stiff, middle-finger salutes of other drivers. And there, in the middle of the road, would be some wondrous treasure. You would dart out into the highway and retrieve the item, perhaps a suit jacket. Upon returning to the car, you would dust it off and proudly display the booty. "Pierre Cardin," you would announce, fingering the material with a show of judicious approval — and somehow it would be relatively new and always your size.

Your acuity for finding road kill appeared, at times, almost supernatural. Once, on a trip from Prescott, Arizona to Southern California, you announced as we pulled out of the driveway that you were going to find a Navy pea coat. Even for a man of your well-documented talents, this seemed to border on hubris. At the time I was twelve, pissed off about the divorce, and not inclined to forgive your foibles. So as the miles wore on and no pea coat appeared, I ribbed you mercilessly. But you took this in stride, insisting with good-natured assurance that the trip wasn't over. And damned if after two days of travel, not ten miles from our destination, you didn't let out a war cry of triumph and slew the car to a stop, half-blocking one lane of a busy highway. You popped out of the driver's seat, went running back along the median, and when you returned — cocky bastard — you were holding . . . yes, you guessed it, a brand-new, navy-blue pea coat — the kind with a double row of shiny silver buttons down the front. Just what you had ordered. My only consolation was that in this one rare instance, as I recall, it was slightly too tight in the shoulders.

When I was seventeen, we were riding along Interstate 80 somewhere between Berkeley and Oakland, one of the most heavily traveled roads on the West Coast, and you saw a logging chain in the median. You swerved to the shoulder, and a second later, I was watching in horror as you dodged across five lanes of thick, fast-moving traffic to retrieve the chain. It took you twenty minutes and a dozen tries to make it back to the car, and twice I was sure that you were going to be mashed to a pulp by an oncoming semi-truck.

Okay, it was a nice length of chain — but really?

Once, we were in a high-class restaurant in Sausalito, and you were sitting right in front of the dessert table. All through dinner, you kept turning in your chair and eyeing the cakes. There was one particularly delicious-looking chocolate cake that had been completely consumed — with the exception of a single tall, triangular piece with a three-inch mound of crumbs and frosting heaped to one side of the platter. As I knew you would, after the waiter had cleared our plates and we were waiting for the check, you leaned back, pinched up a big mound of the crumbs, and ate them. "Delicious," you pronounced.

I hissed at you to mind your manners, and you just laughed — a big, self-assured laugh — and said in a booming voice that carried throughout the small room, "You think that's bad, you should have seen my father." Everyone in the restaurant was watching; they'd all seen you. I was hiding my face in one hand, melting into a puddle of embarrassment under the table. And what did you do? Yep. You reached back, scooped up a fat slab of sticky chocolate frosting, popped it into your mouth, and licked your fingers.

The "Keen Way" was not confined, however, to the simple acquisition of questionable items by dubious means. Later in life it included activities like stowing away on a cruise ship (just to see if you could do it) and bringing a gram of hash back from Turkey (this must have been just for "fun," because as far as I know you never even smoked it).

And what boggles my mind now is that never once did it seem to occur to you that there might be anything even slightly suspect about your actions. Quite to the contrary, all of these incidents were carried out with loud, bombastic pride. But see, the thing was, you were big — big faults, big virtues, big voice, big personality, big smile. You had such charisma, such easygoing charm, that often while my sister and I were cringing in the wings, wishing the ground would swallow us up, other people were captivated by your offbeat behavior.

Your brash self-confidence, unsurprisingly, did lead to some truly boneheaded screw-ups. And the consequences of some of your thoughtless acts could have been disastrous — I mean, didn't you see *Midnight Express*, for Christ's sake? But even when some monumental mistake came crashing down around your ears, were you repentant? Hardly! "Often wrong, but seldom in doubt," you'd laugh. "It's the Keen Way, son."

This didn't always make you easy to live with, but it let you live life on your own terms. You took chances; you didn't give a good goddamn what anyone else thought, and you didn't care who knew it. When I was little, you used to question me, sometimes harshly, and more than once I justified my actions by saying, "Well, all the kids at school do it," to which you would invariably reply, "If all the other kids jumped off a cliff, would you jump off a cliff too?"

From the moment I could think, you taught me to think for myself. You demanded I question authority — although you might have wished I hadn't applied that principle to you quite as assiduously as I did. You insisted I strive for excellence and were adamant that I value my own judgment over that of the herd. In college, Socrates' perennial question, "Which do you value more, the opinion of one wise man or that of ten thousand fools?" settled into my heart like an old friend.

At least some of your self-assurance and don't-give-a-damn attitude rubbed off on me. From an early age, I had a strong sense that normal societal conventions simply didn't apply to us Keens. What my peers perceived as hard-and-fast rules that had to be obeyed, I viewed as artificial constraints to be examined and, based on my own judgment, be accepted or rejected without regard for what other people might think.

This didn't make me particularly popular in school. Nor has it always made life easy. But it has made it interesting. The way you lived, your example of the Keen Way, gave me a sense of freedom, the confidence to step outside the lines, the conviction to do what I thought best even when my friends (and sometimes you) thought I was nuts.

Without that, I wonder if I would have had the courage to build my cabin, go back to college as an older student, quit a high-paying corporate job, or homeschool my children. So . . . even though I was embarrassed by your quirky habits when I was a kid, resentful of being so different as a teenager, and more than once just plain pissed off at you as an adult; despite the fact that when I read this to my wife, she guffawed loudly at the thought of me chiding you for a lack of manners (as she maintains I have none), looking back, I wouldn't have it any other way.

And I suppose this is my own expression of the Keen Way.

# chapter 11

# Dionysus in '69

*A man needs a little madness, or else . . . he never dares cut the rope and be free.*

— Nikos Kazantzakis

**SAM:** During a decade-long pilgrimage through a maze of academic hallways at Harvard and Princeton, I managed to accumulate an S.T.B. (Bachelor of the Science of Theology), a Th.M. (Master of Theology), and a Ph.D. (Doctor of Philosophy). After graduation and a few temporary teaching jobs, I accepted a position at the Louisville Presbyterian Seminary as Professor of Philosophy and Christian Faith. So, shortly before you turned two, we packed up our worldly goods in an old '53 Chevy and moved from Princeton, New Jersey to Louisville, Kentucky.

In the beginning, I was enamored of everything about my new profession: the role, the costume, and the ritual. In short order I accumulated three suits (including one black three-piece fit for a banker), four tweed jackets, an assortment of slacks, enough ties to hang a regiment, and one orange-and-black-striped Princeton Tiger robe for formal occasions. Those were the ancient days before casual Fridays, so professors were expected to dress in a professional manner at all times. So dressed, I walked a little taller and swaggered just enough to signal that I was to be addressed as Dr. Keen.

My professional life blossomed, but I was busy and had little time for you or the family. I became one of the most popular professors on campus and a neglectful father.

During this period, I continued to question Christian dogma and develop a rebellious attitude toward authority. The majority of my students respected me for this, and I had a special relationship with a handful of students who were on fire to learn. They made teaching a privilege. It was to my house they flocked for comfort when President Kennedy was assassinated. They came to me for support when they marched with Martin Luther King, Jr. and did hunger fasts on the steps of the State House.

I felt satisfaction in my profession because it was my obligation as well as my delight to be critical of unexamined claims, to question, question, question. Suddenly, breaking Mother's taboo against skepticism was a requirement, and I was freed from the demand that I possess answers to the great existential inquiries. I became a joyful practitioner of the discipline of doubt. I was in full agreement with Soren Kierkegaard, who said, "If God held truth in one hand and the striving after truth in the other, I would choose striving after truth."

But right from the beginning, there were tensions and intimations of conflicts to come. In the 1960s, the protests against the war in Vietnam, the psychedelic revolution, and the hippy experiment combined to create a radical atmosphere in American culture at large and a revolution in theological thinking. Liberation theology was making common causes with Marxist revolutionaries in South America and the civil-right movements in the United States. The cover of *Time* magazine asked: IS GOD DEAD?

I embraced the radical mood and offered seminars in existentialism, the death of God, and the philosophy of religion. I joined a group of faculty and students that picketed every Monday on the steps of the post office to protest the war in Vietnam. When the civil-rights movement exploded in Kentucky, I marched with Martin Luther King, Jr., and was disappointed when the police kept us walking in circles most of the night instead of arresting us. As a new professor, I had to publish or perish; my first book, *Apology for Wonder*, was named by both *Time* and *Newsweek* as one of the ten most influential books in the field of religion, and I was designated one of the leaders of the Death of God movement.

Predictably, none of this endeared me to the more conservative members of the seminary. Presbyterians, by their own admission, were supposed to do everything "decently and in order," so the administration and many of the faculty were less than pleased by my playing devil's advocate. One day the president of the seminary called me onto the carpet for a little talk. He began by asking if there was any truth to the rumor that a delegation from one of my classes had requested that I follow the tradition of opening class with prayer.

"I told them that if they did their homework, they didn't need to pray, and if they didn't, prayer wouldn't help them."

The president wasn't amused, and asked me to speak more favorably of such traditional doctrines as the divinity of Christ and the substitutionary atonement.

"We're happy that you are teaching the students to question, but we feel that you should give them answers," he told me.

"I don't have the answers," I replied. "That's why I pose the questions."

Our conversation ended with the warning that he had received complaints about my conduct, and he asked that I be more cautious in my public presentations. But I knew my popularity with the students would protect me from dismissal. So I disregarded his advice and continued to teach as I pleased. But from that day, I began to suspect I could not remain a seminary professor. I had gone too far in the quest for intellectual freedom to pay lip service to orthodoxy, and I found the pious atmosphere in seminary inhibiting.

They considered me dangerously radical, but I knew my spirit was still far too tame.

Fortunately, in 1969 I was due to begin a sabbatical leave, a year of Jubilee. For the first time in nineteen years, since I had entered college, I would not be caught up in the single-minded pursuit of my profession. I expected the year would be a time of creative renewal and taking stock. I had no premonition how radical the changes would be.

When the semester ended, my students gave me a button that said DIONYSUS IN '69, the whole family climbed into our modified VW bus, and we headed to California so I could study humanistic psychology and the New Age therapies that were blossoming as prolifically as crabgrass.

When we landed in Del Mar, we plunged into a sea of new possibilities. I went to my first encounter group with the philosopher Abe Kaplan. In the course of revealing how lonely I had been when my father disappeared on his long trips, I exploded into orgasmic grief and experienced the difference between allowing myself to be spontaneously moved by my feelings and my usual academic style of analyzing emotions.

The whole family attended a seminar with the famous psychotherapist Virginia Satir. She had you and me act out a scene, typical of the frustrations we both felt, in which I came home tired after work, flopped in a chair, and tried to read the paper. You keep disturbing me, trying to get my attention, until I exploded and yelled, "Leave me alone." You left feeling hurt, and I returned to the paper feeling guilty. Virginia made a slight change in the script in which I made physical contact with you, and I said, "Gif, I'm tired, but if you let me read the paper for ten minutes, I'll give you my full attention. Would that be all right?"

And you replied, "Sure, okay, Dad."

This was our first lesson in dissolving conflict and my coming to terms with my habit of ignoring you.

Our apartment was right on the beach, and I bought an eight-foot-long, yellow surfboard — Moby Banana — that was out of style among the younger surfers but just the right heft for a professor. Every morning when you left for school, I went surfing, and it wasn't many days before I could catch the easier waves.

No sooner was school out than you arrived at warp speed to join me. It was the first time in your life that I had ample free time to spend with you. And when we began surfing together, it created a steady father / son bond that we had previously experienced only intermittently. I remember one day, paddling side by side, trying to catch a large wave. You caught it, and I missed it. My immediate reaction was . . . *son-of-a-bitch*. It was the first time I remember you surpassing me. I was surprised, and I felt both proud and envious.

When I think back on these two idyllic years in Del Mar, I've often wondered if our relationship might have blossomed sooner had we stayed there.

It was a wonderful time of freedom, and among other assorted activities, I ended up writing a few articles for *Psychology Today*, which was published in Del Mar.

One sunny afternoon, I dropped into Bully's, a dark bar-bistro across the street from *Psychology Today*, to have a leisurely, solitary lunch. The people in the booth next to mine, whom I could hear but not see, were talking about an article they had just gotten, and someone said, "I wish more of the articles we received were this well written. Who is this guy Sam Keen?" My ears perked up. I was astounded. These professional writers and editors were talking about my work!

At that moment, I heard a still, small voice inviting me to become a writer.

By the end of my sabbatical year, I was ready to trade my secure, tenured professorship for the excitement of freelancing, so I called the seminary and said I wanted to resign. As it happened, the faculty was returning from their lunch break, and within an hour they called back and accepted my resignation. Because of my disturbing habit of asking questions that suggested I was no longer a Christian, I wasn't surprised by the speed of their decision. At the time, I was in the apartment in Del Mar by myself. I was so ecstatic that I sang for hours at top volume, and could scarcely talk the next day.

I was my own man. I mean *free*.

– chapter 12 –

# The Wristwatch

The ocean has only one taste, the taste of salt.
Truth has only one taste, the taste of freedom.

— The Buddha

**GIF:** The first true love of my life was the Pacific Ocean.

We moved to Del Mar, California in 1968, shortly after I turned eight. At the time, Del Mar was a quiet haven for hippies, surfers, and overweight, Republican retirees, just one of the sleepy, slightly rundown little beach towns with names like Carlsbad, Cardiff, and Encinitas, stretching north of San Diego like a string of tarnished pearls along a poorly maintained, two-lane highway. We arrived on a hot summer day, my parents, my sister, and I, all crammed into our decrepit VW bus. Cranky, tired, and uncertain what we would find, we wound our way past a collection of artsy shops dotting the main road, curved down a long hill toward the ocean, and eventually parked on a potholed lane behind the two-story, clapboard beach house that was to be our home for the next year.

Bursting from the car, I ran to the narrow spit of sand that made up our new front yard. Not fifty feet from the front of the house was a short, concrete seawall and beyond that, a broad, white, sandy strip of beach lined with palm trees and modest houses. There were surfers and sailboats and people walking along the water's edge, dogs frolicking in the sand, children flying kites.

But all I could see was the ocean.

Standing there, bare feet rooted in the sand, my heart flew from my body, drawn into vast, limitless blue. Some long-dormant yearning stirred, then thundered awake, kindling strange, potent emotions for which I had no words.

The surf was up that day, and big, glassy waves were running along the shore, their blue-green faces rippling in the sun as they collapsed into froths of white foam, then marched toward the beach in stately, even rows. And past that, the Pacific stretched out, out, out beyond sight, beyond knowledge, beyond imagination.

Overwhelmed, I closed my eyes and listened to the bass roar of the pounding surf, the hiss of the whitewater as it pushed up the beach, the lull as it receded. I heard the cry of gulls and the soft, friendly rustling of palm fronds. The breeze caressed my face, carrying the scent of the sea, of salt, of exotic vegetation and distant lands.

It tasted of freedom.

My love of the ocean only grew in the days that followed. The sound of the surf rocked me to sleep, and the smell of salt greeted me each morning before I opened my eyes. I swam in the ocean every day, and spent every moment I could on the beach.

All too soon, school started, but each afternoon, I would hurry from the bus, kick off my shoes, don a pair of ragged shorts, and run for the water.

To the north, the land was flat, running right down to the ocean, and the beach was crowded, lined with deck chairs, tattered beach umbrellas, and dilapidated boardwalks. I could only go half a mile before the sand died into a tall, dirt bluff, too steep to climb, with jagged rocks barring further passage.

But to the south, only a short way from the house, cliffs rose high above the ocean, the houses disappeared, and few people explored the terrain. The beach stretched on and on for miles, beckoning, promising mystery and adventure. But sadly, it was denied me.

At least at first.

Like any curious eight-year-old, I wanted to wander, and like any responsible parent, Mom worried. Initially I was required to stay within sight of the house. Before long, I was allowed a touch more freedom but was still prohibited from going past the first point, which was a quarter-mile from the house. This way, if Mom got worried, she could walk out to the beach and find me or call me in for dinner.

But beyond that point, the beach grew wild and empty. Half a mile farther, there was a whole series of tide pools. You'd taken me there a couple times, but you were always in a hurry, and I'd never had a chance to explore. I could just see the edge of the pools from the limit of my permitted range, and they called to me with an irresistible siren song.

And so, quite predictably, there came an afternoon when I gave in to temptation. Casting an anxious glance over my shoulder, I jogged down the beach. The tide was out, and the tide pools were vast expanses of wonder. I explored pool after pool, clambering over the algae-slick rocks, slipping into the water, soaking my clothes, and scraping my knees. There were brilliant sea anemones, their multicolored tendrils waving in the water. Sea urchins with poisoned spines lodged themselves in the interstices of the rocks. I saw an octopus, an eel, and innumerable fish.

Suckered by the thrill of illicit adventure, I lost track of time. It wasn't until the sun turned to a molten ball and began to quench itself on the distant horizon that I realized the hour. Quickly quitting the maze of tide pools, I made my way to the hard strip of damp sand at the water's edge and began running back along the beach.

I should have been home half an hour ago. Mom would be looking for me. By now, she might have sent you after me. I picked up the pace, praying I could make it back to the safety of my permitted zone. But I was well short of the point when I looked up and saw your unmistakable silhouette jogging down the beach toward me. A thrill of dread dropped into my stomach like a bad burrito.

I was about to be in a world of trouble.

"Your mother's looking for you," you said when we met. "Where've you been?"

"I know I wasn't supposed to go beyond the point, but the tide was so low and the tide pools were so cool. I'm sorry; I won't do it again."

Head bowed, I waited for the ax to fall.

"Come on," you said, a repressed smile plucking one side of your mouth. "We don't want to be late for dinner."

We walked back together in the failing twilight, side by side, watching the clouds fade from orange and pink to purple and finally grey.

The expected punishment never came. Instead, the next day you gave me a watch. It was a small, cheap Timex with a white face, black hands, and a thin, black-leather band, wrapped in a hard, plastic box emblazoned with the logo TAKES A LICKING AND KEEPS ON TICKING.

You and Mom had discussed it, you told me — your eyebrows beetled downward in a way that left little doubt as to the kind of conversation it had been. Although it wasn't explicit, I understood that she wanted to keep me on a short tether, but you had overruled her. The upshot was that from now on I would be allowed to walk on the beach whenever and as far as I wanted. There would be only two restrictions.

First, I was not to cross the slough at Torrey Pines. This was a huge, swampy inland bay fed by a narrow inlet from the ocean. Depending on the tide, the channel to the slough could range from a thin, knee-deep trickle that was easily forded to a wide, deep race that could sweep a strong swimmer half a mile out to sea, or even worse — if the tide was coming in — drag a small boy into the morass of the slough, where he would sink into the mud and disappear forever.

But this was hardly a hardship. The slough was four miles from the house, a world further than the tide pools that had been off limits the day before.

The second restriction was that I was to take my new watch and be home no later than six. This was a big responsibility, you told me — but you thought I was ready for it. If, however, I was late, even one time, you would take back the watch, and my new privileges would be rescinded.

The watch became a talisman of awesome power. It granted me respite from stifling oversight and left me free to commune with the ocean. That watch and I walked hundreds of miles together, and oh, the things we saw.

After storms all sorts of detritus would wash up on the beach, inciting fantasies of shipwrecks and desert islands. I became a regular denizen of the tide pools, and collected hundreds of shells that sat neatly arranged on my dresser. There was a cave in the cliffs that became my hideout; there were long, steep banks of ice plant that I could roll down, then wash off the thick, gooey sap in the ocean. Many days, I walked all the way to the slough, and except for the occasional surfer or desultory beachcomber, once past the tide pools I was often alone, ruler of my own kingdom.

Once that summer, I saw a beautiful young woman lying naked on the beach, eyes closed, back arched, hand working between her legs. She never noticed me, or maybe she did and didn't care, but as I walked past, flushed and mesmerized, I saw everything. She even had red pubic hair. Wow.

I wondered if, on that long-ago evening when you found me sneaking back from my illicit trip to the tide pools, wet, bedraggled, and filled with excitement, you thought back to the hours you'd spent roaming the woods with your brother. I imagine now you were perhaps a little proud of me for pushing past the limitations Mom had set. In any case, you granted me independence, and it was one of the most wonderful periods of my childhood.

As I remember, I was never once late — and I never did cross the slough. I wanted to, and a couple of times when the water was low, I was tempted. But you had given me the twin gifts of trust and freedom. I was grateful, and for the first time, genuinely wanted to respect your wishes.

Sometimes I wonder if we'd stayed in Del Mar, perhaps that embryonic trust would have developed into real respect, and we might have become friends many years sooner. But a year later, you tore me from the beach, transporting me to the harsh realities of divorce, redneck schools, and the high, dry desert of Arizona so very far from my love — the sea.

Still, that brief idyllic time had a profound effect on the man I became. The memories of the ocean and the person I had been, walking along the beach, sustained me through the dark times that were to come. In later years, those memories inspired many of the most foolish and wonderful decisions of my life. With that cheap little Timex, you bought me a long, sweet, dangerous taste of freedom, a taste I have never forgotten.

And there is no greater gift a father can give his son.

# chapter 13

# Siren Song

Sometimes a man stands up during supper
and walks outdoors, and keeps on walking,
because of a church that stands somewhere in the East.

And his children say blessings on him as if he were dead.

And another man, who remains inside his own house, dies there,
inside the dishes and in the glasses,
so that his children have to go far out into the world
towards the same church, which he forgot.

— Rainer Maria Rilke

**SAM:** While I was still on sabbatical, and shortly before I resigned from the seminary, I accepted an invitation to teach a month-long seminar on "Theology and the Human Potential Movement." Heather and I made the pilgrimage to Esalen Institute in Big Sur — ground zero for exploring the human potential, spiritual awakening, and nude bathing in hot tubs perched high above the pounding Pacific.

I was both titillated and anxious about the nudity and the permissive atmosphere. Heather and I were suffering the twice-seven-year itch and were none too happy with our marriage. I hoped I would be led into temptation and delivered from inhibition. From puberty onward, sex had been a persistent, ubiquitous urge. The siren song of the flesh waylaid me, and the strength of its appeal grew in direct proportion to its level of taboo.

By the second day at Esalen, our inhibitions had melted enough to dare the descent into the baths. As nonchalantly as possible, we undressed, leaving towels around our waists until we could slip into the communal tub to survey the field of naked bodies displayed before our wondering eyes. Almost immediately, my gaze fixated on one of the most stunning women I had ever seen — not that I had seen many naked women during my years as a professor of philosophy.

She (may "She" and "Her" be capitalized, but remain anonymous to protect Her innocence or guilt) was sunning Herself on one of the massage tables. Her body shone in the early morning light, perfect as my dreams of archetypal beauty. Her face was rounded and might have been soft except for the deep lines on Her forehead and thin lips pulled tight under the jurisdiction of Her willpower. Her hair was a mixed bouquet of wild daffodils and meadow grasses that She brushed and tended as frequently as a banker might check a stock portfolio. There was something regal, perhaps arrogant, in Her bearing that suggested that one should approach ready to do Her bidding, grateful to receive Her favors. It is no exaggeration to say that Her beauty hypnotized me. When She was anywhere within my panorama, my eyes flew to Her as a moth to a flame.

During our month at Esalen we talked and flirted, but kept a safe distance.

When the month was over, I left Esalen, still married with children, too old for an Indian Summer of Love, still troubled by erotic fantasies, still in thrall to vague feelings of shame.

After Heather and I returned to Del Mar, we were offered, and accepted, jobs at Prescott College in Arizona, Heather teaching dance and me philosophy of the person. I had no idea at the time that this move would be so disastrous for you, but I was powerfully drawn to Prescott. We had visited Dad there during the last years of his life, and he was buried in a small cemetery overlooking the town. For me, it was holy ground. Dad was everywhere and nowhere, homogenized into the flaming aspens, the vast horizon of Antelope Valley, the redolent, musky wool of Navajo rugs in trading posts. Everywhere I went, he wasn't. In ways I did not understand at the time, I had to return in order to leave.

Soon after we moved into a little ranch house nestled among the boulders on the outskirts of Prescott, Heather and I began to talk about having an open marriage. Most likely, nothing would have come of our fantasies. But one ordinary September afternoon, out of the blue, summoned only by the power of our erotic imaginations, She, the beauty from the baths at Esalen, appeared at our front door without even a warning phone call. Over the next week, we played out some of our fantasies. It was awkward, tentative, and strangely innocent. When it came time for Her to leave, Heather agreed I should visit Her next time I went on one of my frequent business trips.

You kids didn't understand what was happening, but the affair made you anxious. Both Heather and I assured you that everything would be fine; we weren't getting divorced. And we meant it. It seemed at the time no more than an innocent exploration. We had no idea the havoc it would cause.

The details of how She and I flirted, courted, and finally cohabitated are not relevant. Ours was a seemingly perfect union of opposites, a circle and a line that encompassed the geometric possibilities of time. Our aesthetics were ideal: She, a ripe California apricot; me, a Tennessee blue-tick hound. We were an item. Others imagined we were the incarnation of passion. In sad fact, we were more intimate warriors than lovers, each trying to win a victory over spectral forces that ruled the chthonic kingdoms of our separate underworlds. Sex was a part of our struggle, not a respite. There was much scorekeeping, counting of erections and orgasms, both of which fell short of the advertised norm as reported by *Cosmopolitan* and *Playboy*.

Nothing more eloquently describes the chaotic climate of our relationship than the statistics of our movements. In twenty-four months, we shared living spaces in four cities for a grand total of eight apartments or houses, one Airstream trailer, and countless motels. Our domestic life — if it can be called that — was punctuated by continual flare-ups; a dozen transcontinental trips with rendezvouses in New York, Washington, Phoenix, and San Francisco; and three psychedelic journeys beyond the bounds of ordinary reality.

In spite of my obsession — I could go no more than a few minutes without thinking of Her — I was strangely unresponsive to Her body.

Night after night I lay next to Her, mostly impotent and ashamed, unwilling to flee the erotic cauldron in which I believed the alchemy of my transformation would take place. No matter what the cost, I resolved not to let my father's taboo cripple my life.

I remember only a single night when we lay silently and contentedly by a fire, listened to the rain, and fell asleep fused into a single body. It was only in dreams that we shared the intimacy for which we longed. In spite of Her extraordinary beauty, it was not the carnal woman with whom I fell in love. It was not sexual ecstasy I was seeking but the freedom of my own body.

By the time our affair ended, I understood that for me it had been, fundamentally, an act of rebellion in which I'd refused to live in the shadow of my father. I was determined to take up his uncompleted destiny: the exploration of sexuality and the unwavering commitment to vocation.

– chapter 14 –

# The Alarm Clock

It is always consoling to think of suicide:
by means of it one gets through many a dark night.

— Friedrich Nietzsche

**GIF:** In 1972 you left the family for good.

Mom bought me an alarm clock.

And that year I thought constantly about killing myself.

When we moved to Prescott, Arizona, in the fall of 1970, I felt I'd been cast from Eden directly into hell. We'd previously been living in Del Mar, only yards from the beach. There I had embraced the free-spirited, wild sixties with all my naïve, preadolescent heart. I let my sun-bleached, surfer-blond hair grow past my shoulders and wore bell-bottomed, gold velour pants trimmed with tied-to-the-side, braided yarn belts of my own devising.

But what had been the height of fashion in Del Mar was greeted with an overwhelming lack of enthusiasm by the sons of white, Republican ranchers in Arizona, a fact I discovered my very first day at Taylor Hicks (no kidding) Elementary. I was immediately ostracized and branded a dirtyhippy — one word in Prescott at the time. To make matters worse, I read at a college level and had a better vocabulary than most of my teachers. For me, California was the ultimate in cool, and Prescott was home to a bunch of ignorant, backwater hicks whose idea of a good time was castrating cattle and inbreeding with their cousins — opinions I was all too eager to share with my classmates. Unsurprisingly, this did not add to my popularity.

But even worse than the bullies at school or even the impending divorce was an overwhelming sense of displacement. In Del Mar I had excelled in school. I fit in. I understood the world and knew I belonged in it. When we moved to Prescott, I was lost.

In our house in Prescott, there was a freestanding fireplace in the center of the living room that had a black, conical, sheet-metal chimney. Soon after we moved in, you had written on it in thick glops of orange, red, and yellow oil paint: A MAN NEEDS A TOUCH OF MADNESS. It was an act of courage, a cry for sovereignty, and it touched something in my soul. I wasn't quite sure what it meant, but I damned well knew I needed a touch of something — and madness sounded pretty good at the time.

Even after you were gone, that quotation from Zorba the Greek remained. I used to wonder if you had left it there for me, a mysterious message that, if I could only decipher its true meaning, would unlock the power I felt must be hidden inside me; it would transform me, magically rendering me worthy of your care.

Then one day I came home from school, and where those bright letters had been, only a discolored swatch of black remained. Mom had painted over it. The last tatters of your courage that remained to me had been erased.

I was furious. But when I confronted Mom, instead of displaying remorse, she presented me with the alarm clock. She informed me that she had been oppressed by men for far too long. She would no longer be a domestic slave, or subservient to the whole dominant, male-chauvinistic culture — for which it seemed, as the only male left in the house, I was somehow personally responsible. The practical upshot was that from now on I was to make my own breakfast, pack my own damn lunches, and above all, use my new alarm clock to get myself up for school in the morning.

Looking back, it's easy to see that Mom was just as lost and angry and afraid as I — her world had shattered, and she was searching for a way to cope. But I was only eleven and didn't understand. In my young, desperate perceptions, it seemed that she, like you, had abandoned me, abdicating care and responsibility. And it was a harsh blow, one that left me feeling cut off from the remaining vestiges of our broken family.

The alarm clock was round with an orange-painted, metal body, a fluorescent-green face, darker green numbers, and hands that glowed in the dark. On top were two half-round, brass-colored bells connected by an overarching metal strap. A brass striker sat between the bells, and there were four small, rounded wire handles on the back — one for winding the alarm, another for the clock itself, and two more for setting the time and the alarm.

Over the next months, I came to despise that clock with incalculable intensity — more than it should be possible to hate an inanimate object. Not only did it become a potent symbol of how my young life had imploded, but it ticked. All night long. During the interminable nights of my fifth- and sixth-grade years, as I lay fighting terror and insomnia and grief, the ticking, almost unnoticeable in the day, filled my ears with a thunderous roar until my very thoughts seemed to grind like the gears of that gaudy green clock — twisting out of control, chasing themselves down the darkest corridors of my mind, running amok — each clack of the little hands a body blow of mortification, a mocking reminder of my myriad inadequacies, of my hopeless situation.

I was terrified of the bullies at school, and, to the accompaniment of the clock, each remembered humiliation of the day was replayed endlessly. I rewound the latest arguments with Mom, imagining what I should have said, or reviewed recent slights from my teachers. Always, eventually, I would get back to wondering about you. Would you come back and get un-divorced? Would you come for Christmas? Would you ever take me away?

In the end, I blamed the torment of those sleepless nights — the depredations of the bullies, Mom's negligence, and especially your absence — all of it, on that goddamned clock.

―――――

Soon after the alarm clock came into my life, Mom and I began a despicable series of power struggles that were not to end for many years. It started with the TV. I had been drugging fear into submission with a daily string of TV shows that started the moment I got home from school and stretched through to bedtime. She decided it was rotting my mind and cut me off. Then I started taking a bus out to the college after school each day and playing pool until it was time for her to take me home. For some reason (perhaps related to me hustling money from the college students), it was decided that this was not an appropriate activity. As an additional insult, I was told I could only play pool if I brought a friend from school with me. But I was an outcast and had no friends. Catch-22.

At last, I gave up and lost myself in books — the only things I knew Mom would never deny me — and spent all afternoon and late into the night reading science fiction, sometimes going through as many as a dozen novels a week. But I lost hope.

That was when I started to think about suicide.

I had a pearl-handled penknife no thicker than my finger but with a blade almost eight inches long. I used to open it and set the point against my chest and imagine plunging it into my heart. I pushed gently a time or two, but it hurt, and I knew I didn't have the courage to stab myself.

I thought for a while of hanging myself, but it seemed so horrible to strangle, gasping for air. Still, I fashioned nooses on lengths of hemp rope I found in the garage, morbidly twisting the long, complicated knots and wondering where I could suspend them.

I dreamed of finding a gun and taking it to school. The first person I'd shoot would be Sherman, the bulky, cruel football player. Then William, with his sharp tongue and pointy-toed cowboy boots that left perfect, round bruises on my shins (and occasionally, when he and his friends knocked me to the ground, on my ribs as well). And after they were dead, when there was no going back, I would put the gun to my head and pull the trigger.

I just wanted the pain, the fear, and the humiliation to stop. I wanted to be dead. I wanted everyone to feel sorry for what they'd done. But I couldn't bring myself to do the deed. I lacked resolve, and I despised myself for it. If only I had the guts to stand up to the bullies, perhaps I wouldn't need to kill myself. Or if I had that courage, perhaps I could find the metal to do away with myself.

And like children do, I blamed myself for your abandonment. I was nothing like the man you had tried to raise. I wouldn't lift a finger around the house; I got bad grades at school and refused to comb my long, unruly hair until knots the size of mice formed along the back of my head. A man, you always told me, had to be strong and fearless. Yet I was small for my age, and weak. I was terrified all of the time.

In the end, I do not know which was more debilitating: the fear that it was my own cowardice, my lack of a work ethic, or my small stature rendering me unworthy of your love, or the sick knowledge that it had nothing to do with me, that I could have been a cross between Paul Bunyan, Muhammad Ali, and Jesus Christ — and still you wouldn't have wanted me.

So many things about that period of my life are unclear, lost in a haze of depression. Did I really call you on the phone, not once, but many times, and beg you to please, please, please take me back to California? Did I really tell you that I knew why you'd gone — but for God's sake, to please not leave me there in that living hell? Or were these only imaginary conversations that I replayed over and over as I lay tossing in bed, kept awake by that damned clock, until I finally believed they had really happened?

I don't know.

When you left the family and returned to California with your lover, the worst part was that I could hardly blame you. I was half in love with her myself, as only a twelve-year-old could be, and I knew I wasn't much of a prize. Hell, if I had been you, I would have traded me for her in a heartbeat.

And besides, I would have done anything to get out of that house, away from the rednecks in Prescott, back to California.

So, really, I understood why you left. But why didn't you take me? That's what was so hard to bear at the time. And now, as a father to a boy of my own, it seems even more incomprehensible.

At first I was hesitant to dredge up old memories and write about this difficult period so long past. But no honest account of our journey can ignore your abandoning me. It was perhaps the most formative event of my childhood and, more than any single experience, has shaped the way I relate to my children. Although it is an appalling story of the very worst part of my life, I hope it can prove cathartic for you. After all, you lived with the fallout of those years for many decades. I punished you for that abandonment, without a trace of compassion as only one who feels himself a victim could.

Perhaps I thought you should know why.

– chapter 15 –

# Farewell My Father, Farewell My Son

*Only in the agony of parting do we look into the depths of love.*

— George Eliot

**SAM:** Over Christmas, 1971, She and I traveled to Prescott for the holidays. This was a painful and confusing period. The marriage was over, but the divorce was still to come. I was in and out of the house, sometimes with Her, sometimes alone, sometimes staying in a small Airstream trailer in the driveway. Nobody knew what was going on.

She and I had no sooner arrived than the liturgy Heather and I had created — tea and oatmeal cookies, vegetable soup and fresh bread — overwhelmed me. Lael began her chronicle of the doings of her animals — Amelia Rabbit, who disappeared into her burrow at the first sign of snow; and Rat, who was charming as ever but given to petty thievery.

You punctuated the silences between every sentence with a demand that I inspect the site you had chosen for a fort. Longing for a stolen moment with you, I let you take me by the hand and lead me out onto the hill from which I would later quarry my father's gravestone. We climbed over boulders and skirted brush tangles to a spot where three large rocks formed a semi-cave. Inaccessible from three sides and not even visible from the house, it was large enough for two to sleep in and contained space for a fireplace in which to cook bacon. A small plateau overlooked the valley and provided a strategic place to dry-gulch any approaching enemy. We, co-architects, created our blueprints in the sky and planned to return the next day. But the mania for building had gone too far to be postponed. "If you get the ax and shovel," I said, "I'll start clearing the fallen rocks, and we can get a good start before supper."

You hurried off. The pine-scented wind swirled around me, and for a moment I was also eleven years old. While you were gone, I gathered boulders and placed them to create a wall. By the time you returned, we were ready to cut the saplings that would form the walls. We heaped old brush outside to add strength and camouflage to render the fort invisible. As darkness fell, we sat back and admired our handiwork. Then, hand in hand, with a fleeting, warm feeling of camaraderie, we made our way back to the house for dinner — the house that would never again be my home.

That night sleeping beside Her in a rented room, all I could do was think of the unfinished fort and wonder if you and I would have time to build a life together before you made a home of your own. But all the while I was being swept along by a tide that was carrying me further and further from home. The paradoxical possibilities assaulted me like a series of tornados coming together to create a perfect storm. Night and day, I was obsessed. I couldn't stop thinking about my lover or my family, and there were times when the swirling, impossible contradictions drove me near the shoals of insanity.

The day before I finally left Prescott, abandoned the family, and returned to Del Mar to live with Her, I felt compelled to enact a strange ritual. I searched the hills in back of our house, found a massive, camel-colored stone, and wrestled it through the brush down to the driveway. I spent several hours in a near trance, with hammer and chisel, engraving my father's name on the stone. Midafternoon, I took it to the cemetery and found the unmarked plot where he was buried near the large juniper tree. I could feel the cold December wind cutting into my flesh and the hot tears making their way down my cheeks.

I excavated a nest in the sandy soil with my bare hands and placed in it a copy of *Apology for Wonder* (which I had dedicated to him) and a pair of worn moccasins he loved that I had retrieved from the hospital room where he died. Then I rolled the stone over the shallow grave. I sat for a long time and shared a bottle of wine with the thirsty earth that was now his abiding place.

Then I spoke my final farewell: "Father, I can't imagine what kind of a man I will become if I do not follow my twisted way. I do not want to look at my life and feel ashamed because I lacked the courage to be myself. Nor do I want to pass on to my children the taboos that you and Mother, with all the integrity of your love, placed on me. For all the chaos and pain I have caused, I ask forgiveness. Forgive me, now, as I forgive you."

Later that same day, She and I left for Del Mar, but we had no sooner reached the Arizona border than I missed my family more than I desired Her. I would willingly have returned. But it was too late. I had set sail on a treacherous journey, lured by an erotic dream of who I might become, and I was destined to be shipwrecked on a barren island. In exile from my family, I could not escape the knowledge that you and Lael and Heather had paid a heavy price for my freedom. For years we were to suffer phantom pains from severed limbs.

– chapter 16 –

# Necklace

In a barren and unhappy time I wanted to share
with my father the burden of my losses,
not the least of which was his grievous absence.

— Stanley Kunitz

**GIF:** The first foreshadowing of reconciliation between us came, oddly enough, at the nadir of our relationship. It was after you had moved out of the house in Prescott but before the divorce, during what I came to think of as the "sock drawer" era.

This innocuous moniker was shorthand for the brief period when you passed through the house at unexpected intervals, for intermittent periods of time, occasionally accompanied by your girlfriend, although at other times alone. And when, sometime during these confusing months, Mom took up with her future ex-husband, I think we knew it was all over but the shouting — of which there was a great deal yet to come.

Whenever you left town to whatever exotic location you and your girl-friend were bound, as if conjured by the vacuum of your absence, my future ex-stepfather would sweep into the master bedroom, bringing with him socks, clothes, and sundries that would magically appear in the recently vacated top drawer of the dresser. When you returned, sweeping in to re-possess your place as father and husband, he would vanish, or at least strategically retreat to lurk in the wings, leaving the sock drawer conveniently empty for your undergarments and toilet kit.

You inherited a love for Native American jewelry from your father, and I inherited it from you. Whenever I could wangle a ride downtown, I would hang around trading posts on the plaza and pester the proprietors with all manner of questions. What little money I could scrape together from generous grandparents, Christmas, or birthdays was hoarded and eventually spent on a ring, some beads, or on one occasion, a turquoise Zuni bear fetish.

Mostly when you came to town, you were distant, preoccupied with the failing marriage, your budding career as a writer, and above all your love life. So I was suspicious when, right around Christmas of 1971, on what turned out to be your last extended occupation of the sock drawer, you took an interest in one of my projects. I had managed to buy a strand of silver beads and was experimenting, stringing them in various patterns, when you suggested that we do something together. On the spot we went out, and you bought a necklace of beautifully polished, round turquoise beads. When we got home, we created two identical necklaces composed of short stretches of your turquoise beads interspersed with my silver beads — one for you and one for me.

Then you were gone again — and this time for good.

But I held on to that necklace. I wore it day and night. I wore it to school, to bed, even in the bath. I never took it off. Over time, the turquoise darkened and began to glow, polished by my sweat. Once, just outside the front door of the house, the necklace snapped. It slid down the inside of my shirt and fell to the flagstone porch, sending beads rolling in all directions. It took hours of searching over a period of five days, but eventually I found all but one.

I still have the necklace today. It sits on my bedside table, and as I write this, I can look over and see one section of turquoise beads, next to the clasp, that is slightly smaller than the others — due to the missing bead.

The necklace was beautiful. But that wasn't why I wore it. It was the associations with you that made it precious. On the eve of your final departure, the depressing finale of the sock-drawer era, you had given me your undivided attention for half of the day (an unheard-of occurrence). You bought the turquoise I coveted, but couldn't afford. Together we designed the necklace and strung the beads. When you walked out the front door for the last time, I could see the alternating pattern of silver and turquoise peeking from the collar of your shirt; you were wearing your half of our shared necklace.

And somehow, in my mind, that necklace became the symbol of an unspoken promise. Even after you were long gone and I was stranded there, shipwrecked in that cold house, even after it became all too clear that you were not going to send for me, I wore that necklace day and night, defiantly displaying it around my neck like a magic claim check, pronouncing to the world that one day — despite appearances to the contrary — you would return to redeem me.

# chapter 17

# Alone

There is only one suffering — to be alone.

— Gabriel Marcel

**SAM:** What happened after I abandoned the family might be summed up as my transition from the Summer of Love to the Winter of Discontent. After leaving Prescott, I returned briefly to Del Mar where She was living — on and off. Then in the winter of 1973, I moved to San Francisco where She was living — on and off. And when She left me (for an unpublished poet, no less), I knew I had to find a way to create a new life from the detritus of the old.

But it wasn't easy. For two years, like a bird with a broken wing, I perched in a bare apartment high on Telegraph Hill surrounded by an odd assortment of orphaned furniture, living in a solitary lighthouse overlooking the dark bay and the Transamerica Pyramid of light. I was alone, and lonely. Nothing to do. No job. No family. No lover. No friends in the city. An astronaut in zero gravity with nothing against which to push.

I tried to be a long-distance father. I phoned frequently and brought you and Lael to San Francisco for school vacations. Lael was always happy to visit, but you were sullen. We went out to dinner every evening and took trips to the beach, but trying to simulate family life in a North Beach apartment was awkward at best. Every time I took you to the airport and watched you get on the plane, my heart broke. Grief mixed with irony; only by losing you did I discover how much I loved you. For the first time, I was not preoccupied with my professional life; I wanted you to live with me.

One day, driving through Richmond, I saw a full-sized billboard that proclaimed: NOTHING MAKES UP FOR FAILURE IN THE FAMILY. It was an instant epiphany. I knew I had to buy a house so I could make a new home, for you, Lael, and myself.

Within the week, serendipity struck. I ran into an acquaintance at a coffee shop, and he began to sing the glories of the nearby community of Muir Beach. It sounded like a place I might settle — ocean-side, small, surrounded by rolling hills.

The next day, after coffee at the Trieste, I went exploring and soon found myself in front of the funkiest house on Sunset Way — one of the two dead-end streets that formed a crescent around Muir Beach. The house was ungainly and large, surrounded by six-foot weeds with a FOR SALE sign in the front yard.

I drove to Sausalito and found the realtor, who told me the owner was somewhere in Spain and wasn't expected back anytime soon. He hinted that the one room with a steel door, bullet holes, and barred windows might have been used to protect a sizable stash of dope, and that the owner's absence was the result of a drug deal gone wrong, potentially having resulted in a life-threatening cash-flow problem.

With little hope of success, I put an offer on the house, and two days later the realtor called. Apparently the owner had returned and was in immediate need of cash! If I could raise ten thousand that day, the owner would carry the balance of the purchase price. That afternoon, without the benefit of banks, lawyers, or loan companies, I became the overwhelmed owner of a house — a large white whale washed up on the beach.

It was to be the beginning of a new life for all of us.

# chapter 18

# Muir Beach

The first duty of love is to listen.

— Paul Tillich

**GIF:** By the time you bought the house in Muir Beach, the surly, maladjusted boy I had been in Prescott had grown into a truly bad-news adolescent. At the time I was living in Boulder, smoking dope, getting brought home late at night by the cops, and flunking out of high school. My struggles with my mother had grown increasingly ugly, and she had no idea what to do with me.

So it was that in the fall of 1976, at the start of my junior year of high school, I came to Muir Beach to live with you, your new wife, and my sister Lael, who had joined you the year before. I still don't know exactly how the decision for me to move to Muir Beach was made, but it was not entirely voluntary on my part, and I was ambivalent about coming to live with you. Boulder had been difficult, but it was still traumatic to be torn from my friends (however disreputable), my school (however despised), and shipped off to you for reformation. Mom had finally found a way to get the better of me, and I arrived brimming with resentment, ready to carry on the battle.

But you disarmed me with a studied indifference. My rebellion was met with an offhand lack of concern, leaving me feeling slightly foolish. Like a wounded bird, you treated me with kindness, surprising compassion, and a healthy dose of respect. In preparation for my arrival, you had constructed a new room, far in the back of the house, complete with its own entrance. What I did in there, you informed me, was my own business. I was allowed to smoke pot in my room. I listened to music at all hours of the day and night.

You went out of your way to make me feel welcome, as if it were really my home. This was a radical concept for me, one I greeted with guarded gratitude and profound suspicion.

But I was at last back in California. Our house was two minutes' walk from the ocean, and Muir Beach was surrounded by miles of rolling hills, dense forests of giant redwoods, and high, grassy ridges filled with deer, foxes, bobcats, and even the occasional mountain lion. I thrived in school and soon had a tight group of friends — many of whom I still know today. They were all stoners, but unlike my friends in Boulder, who would smoke dope then watch TV and talk about cars, this group liked to do things. We would get high, sneak into the back of Muir Woods, and climb high in a giant redwood, or, on a moonlit night, cut the locks on the gates and drive up the fire roads onto Mount Tamalpais with the headlights extinguished so the park rangers couldn't see us.

I cut my hair and started running barefoot through the grassy hills. School was six miles away, on the other side of a steep, windy road; I started biking there five days a week. I showered regularly, and for the first time in my life got into good physical shape.

Given your lenient attitude toward cannabis, and all of the great places to hike, our house soon became a mecca for teenagers. You gave my friends and me the run of the house, and encouraged me to show them hospitality. More than once, my stepmother went ballistic after five stoned teenage boys went through the kitchen like a plague of locusts, stripping the fridge, pillaging the cupboards, devouring everything in their path. But you always stood up for me.

It would be nice to remember this as a time of perfect harmony, but habits die hard, and despite the ease of my new life, our old patterns were deeply entrenched. There were still a hundred little ways we picked at each other, keeping the conflicts alive, but as always, the most pronounced ones were about work. In a time-honored tradition, with steps so often practiced that they were almost automatic, you tried to make me do chores around the house. I resisted, you insisted. I malingered and did a crappy job; you became enraged and belittled me.

The big confrontation exploded one night in front of a sink full of dirty dishes that you had demanded I wash.

"So what are you going to do if I don't?" I asked.

This had been standard fare with Mom. If I didn't do what she wanted, she'd threaten to take away some privilege — and that was where we inevitably ended up. But to my surprise, your answer was something along the lines of, "There's no 'what if?' because you're going to do the dishes. And you're going to do them because it's the right thing — you're part of the family now, and it's only right that you help out."

Then you stomped off, leaving me no way to reengage. I wanted to disregard your argument as guilt-tripping bullshit. But that night it stuck. There were a couple of things that were markedly different. First off, you made an appeal to justice rather than authority. If you had given me the as-long-as-you-live-under-my-roof spiel, I would deliberately have done the worst possible job and then retreated to the jungle to sharpen my spears.

Even that might have been inadequate (I was so entrenched in rebellion, it was a key part of my identity) had you not been treating me so well. You had been showing me genuine respect and going out of your way to accommodate — even encourage — behavior that my mother had been trying desperately to stamp out for the past four years.

So, although it kind of hurt, I did the dishes that night and almost every night thereafter for the next two years. I would like to think I always did them willingly without complaint, but I'm sure I still malingered. The habit was too deeply ingrained. But something fundamental changed that night; I saw the justice of your request because you were willing to respect who I'd become. We still fought and argued and got spectacularly angry at each other, but we made up just as quickly. We didn't hold grudges.

Five years and a lot of hard miles after the divorce, at last the promise of the necklace had been redeemed.

# PART III
# RITES OF PASSAGE

The way to manhood involves an adventure chosen, a risk taken,
a fear faced, and a dream realized.

# chapter 19

# Challenge Discovery

That which does not kill us makes us stronger.

— Friedrich Nietzsche

**GIF:** On June 6, 1974, when I was still living in Boulder, two days before I turned fourteen, Mom dropped me off somewhere near Buena Vista, Colorado with a bag of clothes, a shiny new Swiss Army knife, and a sinking feeling in the pit of my stomach. Since I was too old for summer camp, you had signed me up for a month-long wilderness trip offered through a program called Challenge Discovery. The trip was for kids between fourteen and eighteen, and the first thing I realized was that I was not only the youngest, but also by far the smallest in my troop. I still hadn't achieved seventy pounds, and most of the other kids were twice my weight — or more.

After Mom left, I was given a sleeping bag, some freeze-dried dinners, and a backpack, and told to pack. When I got everything pushed into that orange monstrosity of a pack, I put it on, but the damned thing was so heavy, I took it back off and unpacked it. I couldn't believe what I'd put in it weighed that much, nor could I imagine how on earth I would carry it. The pack probably only weighed forty pounds, but still, it was more than half my weight, I was in crappy shape, and I'd never been athletically inclined.

To add insult to injury, in an act of loving sabotage, you had provided me with a box of Tiger's Milk bars for the trip. You told me to hide them in my pack and only eat one when I really needed it. No doubt you intended this as a kindness, but if I'd had the sense God gave a mule, I would have dumped those things the first day and dropped five pounds from my pack. But instead, I followed your instructions to the letter, and ended up humping them over the Continental Divide three or four times before my fellow sufferers decided to lighten my burden by stealing the damn things, eating them, and shoving the greasy wrappers into my sleeping bag — but I'm getting ahead of the story.

It was midafternoon by the time we left the trailhead. Almost immediately I began to lag behind, and one of the two leaders had to stay with me, chiding me to move faster. Faster, my ass. There was no way in hell I was going to be able to carry that monster pack up the damned mountain. My lungs burnt, my legs felt like noodles, and I thought for sure I would throw up. I had to stop and rest every fifteen minutes. Eventually, though, I fought my way up the trail and broke out above timberline.

Then it started to snow.

I was wearing the wool pants and undergarments specified for the trip (this was before all the nice synthetics) and soon I was soaked, sweaty, and stinking like a dead sheep. At one point I remember finding myself alone on the side of a ridge with snow blowing horizontally. I was so exhausted that I lay down by the side of the trail without removing the pack, content to let the snow cover me. But after a few minutes, one of the leaders showed up, took my sleeping bag, and strapped it on top of his pack, giving me a few not-so-encouraging words (something to the effect that I should get off my lazy ass, quit screwing around, and get up to the top of the damned ridge if I wanted any dinner) before quickly disappearing into the snow.

My load didn't feel lighter, but eventually I did make it to camp. I dropped the pack, ate part of a freeze-dried beef stew, then fell into bed under a makeshift tent constructed from sheet plastic and parachute cord.

When I was shaken awake in the morning, there was a foot of snow on the ground, and I had a bad case of altitude sickness. I was horribly nauseated and couldn't eat. My head felt like someone was driving a metal wedge into my skull. And the worst was an overwhelming lassitude, a weakness in my limbs, a profound disinclination to move. I can't remember ever feeling quite as wretched as I did that first morning.

But of course I had to move. A dozen kids and two group leaders — one man, one woman — were already up and around, eating breakfast, getting ready to go. I couldn't face food, but managed to stuff my sleeping bag and get my pack packed. Once we got started, I was abysmally slow. It was cold, everyone was grouchy, and I was holding up the show. There was lots of complaining.

The stronger kids began to push ahead, and the group started to spread, so the group leaders put me at the head of the line to keep everyone together. We were slogging through knee-deep snow, down the other side of the long ridge we'd climbed the day before, following the footsteps of one of the other groups who had made better time. The whole troop bunched up behind me and made little secret of what they thought of my snail's pace.

Somehow I managed to lose the trail. When this mistake was discovered, the female leader asked me with the utmost scorn how I could possibly have missed a trail of footprints through the snow. The leaders scouted around, found the trail, and let the group move at its own pace down the ridge to the valley below. I was left behind to make my way down the ridge with the female leader walking behind, her silent disapproval washing over me in waves. Eventually I came to a wide valley next to a flowing stream where a couple of the less fit kids had decided to wait. We'd dropped enough elevation that I was feeling better, and ate hungrily. I'll never forget that lunch — peanut butter and honey, squeezed out of Gerry tubes onto Bolton biscuits, a kind of hard, compressed cracker. Plain and unglamorous as it may have been, it was delicious.

After lunch, I managed a good pace, keeping up with the rest of the troop and even passing some of the slower kids. But the damage had been done, and it was that second night, around the campfire, that some of the meaner kids began calling me "Jerkford," a sobriquet that was a harbinger of cruelty to come. We walked for another day, then were trucked to a campground where we were to stay for the next week while learning to climb.

While we had been hiking, the leaders camped with us, and their presence kept the other kids in check. But during our climbing week, they moved their tent to the other side of the river and left us to our own devices. Unfortunately, this left me at the mercy of my troop-mates.

There was one boy in particular — I'll call him Jim — who terrified me. The rumor was he'd shot a man for raping his girlfriend and had been sent on the trip by the courts in Texas in lieu of jail. He was seventeen, big and burly, and liked to pick me up by the front of my shirt, put his face in mine, and tell me he was going to hang me in a tree by my underwear. "That's what we do with faggot hippies down in Texas," he'd sneer. I lived in constant fear of him — absurdly, I think what terrified me most was the possibility that he might discover I didn't wear underwear. Go figure.

I took to eating alone, avoiding the other campers whenever the leaders weren't present, and finding a new, hidden place to sleep every night, far from the campfire.

But oddly enough, during the day, I began to find peace. I'd done some climbing at camp, so I knew my knots. I could belay, and on the rock my slight stature was an advantage. By the end of the week, I was one of the better climbers in our group. Sadly, this did not earn me respect but rather increased my cohorts' enmity.

After climbing, we spent the next week whitewater kayaking. The first few days were a bit dull, floating down slow, meandering streams. But by the end of the week we went to bigger and bigger rivers, and finally worked our way up to some serious rapids. Again, my small size wasn't a hindrance, and I found the whitewater exhilarating.

It's hard to describe the incredible highs and miserable lows I experienced during that trip. The backpacking was so utterly wretched — perhaps the hardest thing I'd ever done physically — and some of the kids were the nastiest little bastards I've ever met. Yet little by little, the beauty of the mountains worked its way under my skin and filled me with a wild elation I had never felt.

I remember when it started to turn around. We had finished kayaking and been bussed to a campground to begin our eleven-day backpacking trip. It was late afternoon, and we were packing, getting ready for an early-morning departure, when Jim came and stood in front of me. He was holding a two-foot length of parachute cord in a loop between his hands.

"Do you know what I could do with this, you little faggot?" he said, a nasty grin spread across his face.

I was tired, and I was dreading backpacking. Here my size would once again be a huge disadvantage, and I could already hear the taunts my slow pace would provoke. They'd pushed me so cruelly for so long, I just didn't give a damn.

"You could probably choke me to death," I replied.

This wasn't what he was used to from me, so he wrapped the cord around my neck and started to squeeze. I stared straight into his eyes until blackness rolled up my vision, and I fell backward, landing on top of two eighteen-year-olds from the other troop.

"Jesus, Jerkford, you klutz," one of them spat at me.

"What a spaz," said the other.

But I ignored them. I got up and stood right in front of Jim again, not saying a word, not doing *anything*, just looking into his face.

"You're a fucking freak," he muttered. But he looked away first and wandered off to pack.

This was hardly the victory of a Hollywood movie, in which I would have beaten him to a pulp — but it was something.

The next week and a half was grueling, worse than I'd expected. The first five days, we walked through relatively easy terrain, but by the end of the week, we began moving into the high country, camping at eleven thousand feet, crossing and re-crossing the Continental Divide. Above timberline, there were no trails in the vast, high landscape, and we soon found ourselves traversing long scree fields or balancing along knife-edged ridges with steep cliffs on both sides. As we climbed past thirteen thousand feet, the air got thin, the terrain grew even steeper, and a remarkable thing happened. Suddenly I found myself in the middle, or sometimes even near the front of our troop. I was a long way from the fastest, but I wasn't the slowest.

On day nine, we were camped on a ridgeline, above twelve thousand feet, when a miracle occurred. Jim, my tormentor, was a serious smoker. He'd packed a carton of cigarettes and had been sucking down a pack a day the whole trip. That night, high, high above the world in a rocky, cold, windblown camp, our tarp tents stretched just below a jagged ridge that fell two thousand feet almost vertically to a lake below, Jim began to wheeze. The wheezes turned to gasps and the gasps to great, wet, hacking coughs.

During the night, he developed full-on pulmonary edema (a gathering of fluid in his lungs). After a worried consultation, the two leaders agreed that they had to get him to a lower elevation. At first light, the male leader roped him up, and the two of them went down a long, steep snowfield to the valley below, leaving the female leader and the rest of the troop to carry on. And just like that, the bastard was gone. By this time, I think the other kids had become ashamed of how they'd treated me; without Jim to whip them up, they left me alone.

We walked all that day along the high ridges, struggling for breath, weaving our way through the scree, stopping regularly to rest. Then, in the late afternoon, we wended our way down a long slope of grassy tundra, out of the rocks, out of the snow, into Rosebud Gulch — a pristine valley by a blue alpine lake so still and deep that the reflection of the peaks in the water was as sharp as the mountains themselves.

After we made camp, I wandered off by myself, far from the group, halfway around the lake to a high promontory of rock with a single fir tree. I sat there for a long time looking at the mountains and the lake and the long, cold waterfall spilling down off the cliffs. I listened to the sounds of water on rock, wind in the trees, and the quiet beating of my own heart. And I was overcome with joy. The beauty of the mountains invaded my body and over-brimmed my heart.

It was one of the most perfect moments of my life.

As dusk approached and ecstasy waned, as it always must, I had a remarkable epiphany. Here I was high in the mountains, more at peace than I had ever been. Yet these were the same mountains in which I had been so miserable. For days I had wished I were dead. But the mountains hadn't changed. So the ecstasy and misery were inside me. Perhaps this seems obvious now, but at the time it was a remarkable discovery. It was this seed that grew into the understanding that no one else could make me sad, angry, humiliated, or even happy. Those choices, those feelings, were mine. They were inside me, not dependent upon external circumstances.

When I got back to Boulder, it was strange. Everything looked the same, but I felt so different. It took me weeks to understand that sometime during the trip, I had stopped being a victim. I didn't even know when it had happened. Was it that amazing evening in Rosebud Gulch when I was first filled by the majesty of the mountains? Was it when Jim choked me almost unconscious, and I came back for more? Was it the long, grueling crucible of miles walked at a high elevation with a heavy pack? Was it the unmitigated, adrenaline-junky thrill of clinging to a vertical rock face high above the canyon floor, or digging in with the paddle, driving my kayak as fast as I could go toward a thundering rapid? Was it the three days of fasting and solitude? Or was it everything put together? I still don't know.

But nobody ever bullied me again.

# chapter 20

# Into the Depths

The brave man is not he who does not feel afraid, but he who conquers that fear.

— Nelson Mandela

**SAM:** Our dive boat was tethered to a 120-foot section of the African Queen that had run aground on Christmas night on the Fenwick Island Shoals off the coast of Maryland. The ragged edges of the wreck moved up and down like the serrated blade of a giant pair of scissors, threatening to rip the hull of our boat if the waves brought us together.

Gifford Warner, the legendary salvage master, had claimed the wreck the moment it had been legally abandoned by the owners who feared liability if oil leaked from the tanks and contaminated the beaches. My brother and I had met Gifford on the docks in Ocean City when he had been looking for divers to help him plug leaks and seal rooms into which he could pump air and, hopefully, refloat the damaged Queen, tow her into port, and reunite her with her previously salvaged larger half. We were immediately attracted to the bearded captain who read the *New Yorker* and talked knowingly about modern literature, so we signed on for the grand sum of fifty dollars per day.

It was six PM on a calm evening in early June. I had been in the water for most of the day, plugging leaks and managing the hoses that pumped air into the tight compartments and into the full-face mask Gifford wore because he had false teeth and couldn't use a normal self-contained scuba mask. My brother Lawrence wasn't with us on this particular day — my first on the job — so I was the sole diver. I was dead tired from the stress of working many hours in the obscure light reflected from the floor of the ocean. I struggled out of my wetsuit and lay down on the deck, where the warm air from the compressor would restore me. By the time Gifford had suited up and was ready to go down through the open cargo hatch into the bowels of the ship, I'd fallen asleep. When I awoke an hour later, I was alarmed to find Gifford still somewhere in the wreck and the air bubbles from his rig breaking the surface in a single spot. By seven thirty, the bubbles' stationary pattern hadn't changed. He wasn't moving. What had happened? Was he injured, dead, stuck in a narrow place?

I was in all kinds of trouble: The compressor was running low on fuel, and I didn't know which five-gallon cans contained gas and which diesel; a lightning storm was making its way toward the boat, which was the highest steel lightning rod in the area; I was twelve miles at sea, in a sixty-foot boat I didn't know how to run; and I had no underwater light and only a couple of partially filled air tanks.

Sweating, I began to devise a disaster plan. I found a flashlight and wrapped it in many layers of clear plastic. I tested the tanks, found the one with the most air remaining, attached a regulator, and found a mask Gifford could use in an emergency.

Up until this time I had never been inside the wreck, so I had no idea where I might find Gifford, or whether he would be injured, alive, or dead. My plan was to trace the faint path of bubbles along the underwater corridors in hopes they would lead me to Gifford. With panic barely under control, I put on a wetsuit, swim fins, and an aqualung, and waddled to the ladder. I paused only long enough to wonder if there might be some way for me to escape the ordeal, then took a deep breath, swung my leg over the railing, and eased a foot onto the dive ladder. As I looked down into the darkest midnight I could imagine, with not even a glimmer of hope to sustain me, I saw a faint light making its way up from the depths. Gifford was returning from the watery underworld! Yes! There was a God!

After we peeled off our wetsuits, got into some warm clothes, and were nursing hot coffee, I asked, "What in the hell were you doing down there for two and a half hours? Your bubbles kept coming from a single location, and I figured you were probably dead."

Gif laughed and fitted a Camel into his long cigarette holder. "I wasn't in any danger. I came up in an underwater room that was filled with air, so I took off my hose and tied it to a railing. Then I started plugging small leaks. I guess I just lost track of time."

Compared to Gifford's normal operating procedure, my ordeal was nothing. As he explained, he often came to the wreck and worked alone. The buddy system all amateur divers used wasn't practical for professional salvage divers because it required two individuals to remain in the water for long periods when there was only enough work for one.

After we recovered from the dive, we headed for the Ocean City marina and home. I didn't stop sweating for three hours.

Several days later, we returned to the wreck to install some wooden doors Gifford had made to close off rooms we were hoping to inflate to float the Queen. This time, having survived my earlier ordeal, I was relaxed and not as vigilant as I should have been. He asked me to take an air hose down and thread it through a hole in the hull where we could retrieve it from inside the wreck. By this time the derelict ship had worked its way deep into the sand, and I had to descend into a narrow trench cut into the ocean floor. Somehow in the process, perhaps when I saw the outline of a real or imagined shark, I lost my grip on the five-hundred-dollar hose; it rapidly disappeared into the murky deep. I returned to the ship deeply embarrassed.

"Not to worry," said Gifford with calm grace. "Let's have lunch and drink a cup of coffee."

That was the last he said about the hose. (Happy to report I found it a week later.)

The serious work began in the afternoon. The wooden doors had to be pulled up the narrow underwater corridors. We manhandled the first door down and through the large cargo hatch. Gif went ahead, up the long corridor, with a rope to pull the door into place. My job was to push from the rear. We were no more than twenty feet into the narrow passageway when I was struck by severe claustrophobia. The walls pressed in on me, and the darkness deepened every foot of the way. I couldn't force myself to proceed. After remaining paralyzed for endless minutes, I turned around and started toward the cargo hatch and the wide-open sky. I was halfway to relief when anger boiled up inside me, and I found myself saying, "No, goddamn it, I am not going to run. I'm not going to let fear get the best of me." With that I turned and made my way back up the corridor. Unexpectedly, facing my fear dissolved the darkness, and I noticed that there was enough light streaming in from small cracks to allow me to see.

Gifford must have known something was wrong, because just as I reached my duty station at the rear of the door, he came bursting into view like some bearded half-god, half-mortal, engulfed in an effulgence of bubbles. He flashed a knowing smile that seemed to me a benediction. I laughed until the water streamed into my mask, and I had to purge it with my breath.

This was the moment I decided that if the child Heather and I were expecting was a boy, we would name him Gifford — the namesake of a brave, kind, adventurous man.

# chapter 21

# Sacred

Your sacred space is where you can find yourself again and again.

— Joseph Campbell

**GIF:** You and I took our first and only psychedelic trip together on a clear summer morning at the farm in Washington, just after I'd turned fifteen. We started the day sitting on the lawn in front of the house, the breeze cool, the sun not quite hot at nine o'clock in the morning. You produced a milky plastic baggy from your shirt pocket and let it unroll, revealing the small, brown, dried psilocybin mushrooms within. We each took a handful, then paused, holding the shriveled caps with their string-like stems in our palms, looking at each other, wondering what the hell we were doing.

Then you cracked a grin. "Chew 'em up good," you instructed me.

And I did.

The mushrooms were dry with a leathery texture and a dark, earthy taste that left a film of pungent dust on my teeth even after I'd chewed, swallowed, and rinsed my mouth with water.

Fifteen minutes later, the drug started to come on.

By that time, we had moved to the back of the house and were sitting on the grass by the creek. I was watching the still, deep pool by the lawn trickle across a wide concrete spillway in liquid sheets then drop off the far side and race down the streambed, chattering as it went. Soon the water started to glisten, crescent-shaped sparks igniting on the surface as the breeze drove sunlight over the pool. The wind rushed through the aspens, their white-barked tops dancing against the sky, the tender green, heart-shaped leaves quivering with delight. My body sunk into the yielding grass; the warm air caressed my skin, evoking imagination of a lover I had never had.

Launched far past the boundaries of dull, ordinary consciousness, I could see individual molecules of air bumping into each other. Every pine needle, every aspen leaf, every blade of grass stood out clear and clean, brought into focus by a miraculous mushroom microscope. I couldn't believe I had been surrounded by such unfathomable beauty all my life and never noticed it.

A giant smile bunched my cheeks as tight as apples.

"Wow," I said.

You were grinning now too, your eyes bright with the drug and the day.

"You want to walk?" you asked.

"Oh, yeah," I replied. "But let's dip first."

We stripped off our clothes and plunged into the pool. Thigh-deep and spring-fed, the water never got much warmer than forty degrees Fahrenheit. I lay down on the sandy bottom and leaned my head back into the icy liquid. Cold squeezed bone deep, like a giant hand. Then, sputtering, I leapt back onto the lawn, skin tingling with frost and fire. We lay naked in the grass, letting the sun kiss us dry, then dressed and started walking.

Across the spillway, through a wire gate and up into the pasture, with joints loose and limbs electrified, a strange, almost nauseous anticipation radiated from the pit of my stomach. Past the knoll at the top of the pasture where five years later I would build a log cabin, we climbed a short, steep forested hill and broke out on a sparsely wooded mesa, where we paused and looked back.

McFarland Creek ribboned out below us, a brilliant band of green threading its way between dry, ponderosa-dotted hills down to the Methow River. We could see the small farmhouse, the barns, the outbuildings, the bright grass, the garden, and the overgrown apple orchard. And suddenly I was struck with an overpowering sense of rightness.

"We belong here too, don't we?" I asked, turning to you. "Humans, I mean."

It was a revolutionary thought. For years, whenever I saw the power lines and the housing developments, the roads and the parking lots, all the devastation that humans cause, I felt like an alien invader, a virus, a blight on the land. But there, looking down on that small farmstead, for the first time in my life I felt connected to the world; I felt like I belonged. My bare feet dug into the soft, dry dirt, toes reaching down to the center of the Earth.

You smiled, then took me by the hand and led me to a tall ponderosa tree standing proudly on the edge of the mesa.

"This is our land, son," you told me. "And when I die, I want you to bury me under this tree, so my spirit can look down on the farm and the valley below. You're right. This is where we belong."

We walked for hours that day, and with every step, we were transported further into wonder. We started up an unused fire road toward Mills Flat, but after a mile we turned up a long stony ridge. Up, up, up we went, talking, laughing, stopping to look at flowers or watch the giant black ravens circle in an azure sky. Finally we came to a warren of rocks on the knobby ridge top, a place I would later come to know as the Dragon's Lair.

We could see forever. The spiky peaks of the North Cascades formed the rim of the world to the west. High above tiny McFarland Creek, we could now follow the Methow River down to the mighty Columbia, a broad, slick strip of steel water lined by a riot of green, cutting through the dry, rolling hills.

Leaning back onto warm rocks, we sat on a pine-needled bench and shared an apple, the bright taste exploding into our mouths, making us laugh with delight.

We stayed there a long time, talking, then sitting in silence, eyes closed, listening to the wind in the pines as the sun slid slowly into afternoon.

We had never been closer.

———

We arrived back at the farm in the late afternoon, tired and starting to come down. The colors began to fade; the crystalline detail of the world began to round; our minds slowed. We drove two miles down the narrow dirt road to the river and swam, the cool water welcome after the heat of the day. Our bodies refreshed and washed of the dust, we went home and ate dinner. Then I slept like the dead.

In the morning I felt heavy, the boundless energy of the day before replaced with sore muscles, the brilliant, translucent colors faded to normal greens and browns, my quicksilver thoughts now slow and torpid, fallen from the stars and stapled to the ground.

But despite the hard comedown, I still remembered that wonderful feeling of belonging, the knowledge that I was a small part of a much greater whole. And I felt a strong connection to you; a bond was forged that day and never again completely broken.

Although far less intense than many of my later trips, the day we took mushrooms together was one of the most profound experiences of my life.

At the time I was fifteen — angry, sarcastic, bitter, and sure I knew everything. Life, I had decided, was meaningless and filled with pain, devoid of honor, joy, truth, or beauty. People sucked. Especially me. I'd lost faith in Christianity early on, and after the divorce, as I watched Mom flit from one New Age guru to the next, I'd become deeply cynical about spirituality. I felt cut off, alienated from myself, my family, and the world around me.

But that small handful of dried mushrooms cracked my heart wide open and let it fill with a radical knowledge of the sacred. Even if I couldn't always see it, I remembered knowing the world as a place filled with unimaginable beauty, waiting just beyond the edge of perception to sweep back and fill me to the bursting point again and again.

That day with you — walking hand and hand, dipping in the pool, standing by the big pine tree on the mesa — changed me permanently and for the better. It shifted my perceptions of the world and planted magic seeds deep in my heart, where they have been growing ever since.

It was also a turning point for you and me. We formed a bond that day: a bond of shared adventure, of trust and respect, a deep, quiet knowledge of the sacred connection between the land and a father and a son.

– chapter 22 –

# A Touch of Madness

Turn on, tune in, drop out.

— Timothy Leary

**SAM:** The '60s were a time of blessed madness and naïve hope that touched each of us in different ways. It was the time of hippies, flower power, Vietnam, Woodstock, altered states of consciousness, the counterculture, Bob Dylan, Ken Kesey, and Carlos Castaneda. Drugs, sex, and rock 'n' roll, baby.

But while the world outside spun wild, the Presbyterian Seminary remained a bastion of moderation. We professors might have one mint julep too many on Derby weekend, but that was as far as the Dionysian spirit of adventure took us.

I was intrigued by the rumors of a new age, but there seemed to be no place to sign up for the revolution. Then, serendipitously, which is the way things happen in the kingdom of psychedelics, I met a university student named Ralph at a party, and he offered me a ticket to ride — first marijuana, then LSD.

As promised, the following Friday he appeared at my front door. We adjourned to the screened porch where he produced three tightly rolled joints, and we lit up. I inhaled again and again and waited for the promised revelation. Nothing happened, although the singing of the cicadae in the velvet darkness seemed louder than normal. Maybe it was bad grass, or maybe my professorial ego was too addicted to control.

Not to worry, Ralph assured me; he had something stronger — LSD — and next week we would trip for sure.

Saturday night next he returned. It was nine o'clock, the children were safely asleep, and I was a bit nervous. But I assumed LSD would be similar to a couple shots of Kentucky bourbon. And Ralph assured me I could always take a Valium and abort the trip any time I wanted.

Wrong!

I took the wafer, plunged down the rabbit hole, and landed on the other side of the mirror. Suddenly everything was unfamiliar. I was filled with swirling sensations. I could see music and hear colors. Everything was charged with promise and erotic energy. I entered a dreamlike state where there was no time, no separation between myself and a rose in a vase on a table, no separation between myself and Heather and the voice of Donovan singing, "They call me mellow yellow."

At first, this psychedelic melting and merging was pure delight, an immersion in a world of wonder in which each object was alive and dense with meaning. But after midnight, the ecstasy faded; I was tired and wanted to return to the familiar boundaries of my ego. I thought that with a little willpower and a Valium, I would soon return to myself. But that didn't work, and the harder I tried, the more panicked I became. I was caught in a mind-maze, a crazy man condemned to wander forever in a dream world where there was no linear sense of time.

After a spell of exile in a bleak, endless eternity, still assaulted by amorphous terror, wondering if I would ever find my way back, I wandered into the bedroom and collapsed.

Eventually, at long last, the images, feelings, and strange personae dropped into a bottomless void, and, exhausted, I slept.

For a year following that first trip, I suffered periodic flashbacks in which I was temporarily overcome by terror, lost in schizophrenia, unable to escape the labyrinth of my own mind. But there was no one in the theological circles in which I traveled with whom I could share the shattering knowledge, the horror, and the beauty I had experienced.

———

My second LSD trip was designed to repair the damage of the first. I had known Wally Panke when we were together at Harvard, and he had recently been put in charge of an experimental program using LSD at Spring Grove State Hospital. When I told him about the flashbacks, he explained that my bad trip was due to having stopped short of clearing the darkness of fear to reach the light of acceptance on the other side. He offered to be my guide on a future trip.

The protocol at Spring Grove was rigid. I was shown into an antiseptic hospital room and given three doses of LSD (in the original Sandoz bottles) over the course of forty-five minutes. I was given eyeshades and attended to off and on by Dr. Panke and a therapist who programmed the music that was designed to lead me on a journey through death and rebirth. It didn't take long to fall into the fearful maze I had experienced on my first trip. I was encouraged to relax and go with it, but evidently I was still unable to get on the other side of ego. I suggested I would emerge from the other side of the looking glass if they would let me go out into the sunlight and sit in the flower garden. But this was not permitted. I was supposed to remain in the place of ego death until I was reborn.

But instead of rebirth, I shattered into three distinct people. For short periods I became a black woman in rural Florida, and later a Polish man who had just been hit by a car and brought to the hospital. But my most lasting reincarnation was as a back-ward schizophrenic upon whom doctors were performing an experiment with mind-altering drugs. I had a paranoid feeling that I was a captive in the hospital and could not escape. Somehow, in a way that made total sense only in the logic of dreams, the essence of my father, the colors of the aspens in Arizona in autumn when he died, the dark hue of his skin and the inordinate love I had for him, were all mixed in with the personalities I had become.

At this point I jumped up, ripped off the eyeshades, and proclaimed loudly, "I don't want to die here. I want to go outside."

I don't remember exactly how the trip ended, but I seem to recall that I refused to put the eyeshades back on, so Wally talked me down and fed me tea and cookies. By the standards of most psychedelic psychonauts, it was a bad trip. I was a failure at allowing the ego to die. But in the end, the worst part of the trip turned out to be the best. I learned I was a control freak; I was chronically, mildly paranoid and self-protective, and kept a lot of emotional distance between others and myself. This insight forced me to become a more open and welcoming man. The bad trip turned out to be a prelude to better things.

# chapter 23

# Cabin

The house shelters daydreaming, the house protects the dreamer,
the house allows one to dream in peace.

— Gaston Bachelard

**GIF:** I graduated from Tamalpais High School in Mill Valley, California on the same day I turned eighteen. Tired of classrooms, teachers, and authority, I had no desire to attend college. The thought of four, six, eight more years of education was morbidly repellant. And for what? So I could get a "good" job and sell my soul a piece at a time to be a lawyer or a doctor or a politician? No way. Not for me. I wanted to live a simple life, opt out, grow my own food, stop participating in a corrupt system that was poisoning the planet and turning people into corporate zombie-slaves.

I was going to be free.

Several of my closest friends shared this vision, and you, in a fit of grand generosity (or perhaps epic stupidity) volunteered to let us take over your farm on McFarland Creek, an idyllic forty acres nestled on the eastern foothills of the Cascades in northern Washington, only a few miles from the Canadian border.

In preparation, I sublet my sister's apartment in Muir Beach, worked through the winter to save money, wrecked the VW Bug you had inherited from Joseph Campbell (and no, I wasn't stoned when I did it, no matter what you've believed all these years), and in the spring of 1979 two of my best friends and I loaded up an old white Toyota truck with our backpacks and a few tools then drove up the center of California, past Mount Shasta, smack through the middle of Oregon and Washington and arrived at McFarland Creek on a cool spring day in April. My girlfriend soon joined us, and the four of us planted a huge garden and spent much of the spring working in nearby apple orchards, thinning small green apples off the overladen branches.

Orchard work sucks. It's hot, brutally hard, and pays peanuts. The pesticides are nasty. But between thinning in the spring and picking in the fall, there was a long stretch of the year when there was no work — which suited us fine. Sure, we were chronically short of cash, but we didn't need much. We had chickens for eggs, goats for milk and meat, and by the middle of the summer, more fresh vegetables than even a horde of hungry teenage boys could consume. For a dollar a gallon, we bought the best fresh milk I've ever tasted — three inches of cream, bring your own jar. Major expenses ran to gas for the truck, tequila, pot, and the occasional grocery run to the health-food store in Lake Chelan, where we stocked up on peanut butter by the gallon, cheese in ten-pound blocks, and plastic-wrapped stacks of corn tortillas three feet high.

So, that first summer, after thinning ended in June, we had time to do whatever we wanted. And what a summer it was. So much happened and so many memories were crowded into such a small space that I still can't believe it was only one season. There were four of us living at the farm full time, but we had an extended group of friends and there were always two or three (or more) visitors. We worked in the garden in the cool of the morning, spent hours swimming in the nearby Methow River in the afternoons, then made huge communal meals that were eaten around a long navy-oak dining table in the kitchen overlooking the creek.

Sometime during that summer I became possessed by the ambition to build a cabin on the property. It may have been you who put the idea into my head. I remember you sitting me down in the kitchen and telling me, "If you build a cabin here on the property, I'll give you some land to go with it, and it will always be yours."

This was a potent symbol of freedom: a house of my own. I would be free to live how I chose and do what I wanted.

If I'd had any idea of how hard it would be to build that cabin, how long it would take, and what it would cost, I doubt if I would have ever begun.

I picked a spot on the side of a knoll at the top of the pasture, and for two hundred dollars, a neighbor drove his backhoe up the road and dug the pad for the house. It would be a moderate size, sixteen by twenty-four feet, with a deck, a pitched roof, and a big bank of windows facing south. To save money I decided to build it from logs, since they could be cut from the surrounding forest.

And so one hot morning in August, with three friends and two chain-saws, I drove down the Methow Valley to Black Canyon Creek. From there we wended our way fifteen miles on bad logging roads back into the mountains until we came to a stand of lodge-pole pines that had been burnt by wildfires some years prior. The trees were dead-standing, devoid of bark and branches, and dry as a bone. They were perfect: straight and light and so hard they rang like a bell when dropped. Moving the logs by hand was a backbreaking process. But after three trips spaced over the next month, they were cut and stacked by the road. The last of my savings went to hiring a dilapidated log truck to come up into the woods and haul them out. It was dead dark by the time we pushed the logs off in a jumble in front of the barn, and I paid off the driver.

Over the next week, I ferried them a few at a time in the back of my pickup up through the pasture; by the middle of September, there was a nice, neat stack of logs sitting next to the construction site. I was ready to begin building. There were only two problems: One, hiring the log truck had exhausted my meager funds; and two, I realized I had only the vaguest idea how to build a log cabin.

Fortunately, apple harvest was right around the corner, and I spent the next six weeks putting away money for the winter.

After picking season, my friends scattered to the winds, promising to return in the spring. My girlfriend and I stayed on for the winter. Snow came in November and didn't melt until April. There was a stretch in January where the mercury didn't push past twenty below for three weeks. At solstice, the sun rose closer to ten than nine thirty. It was down by four, and never peeked over the southern ridge of the creek valley.

By March, we were dead broke — putting three dollars' worth of gas in the truck at a time, adding up groceries in the store and putting half of them back on the shelves. The potatoes we'd put up the fall before and seventy mason jars filled with canned nectarines were all that kept us from going hungry. When Ray Anders, the neighbor, stopped by in early April and asked if I wanted a job, I didn't even ask doing what or how much. I just said yes, then spent the spring installing miles of permanent irrigation. By the time I was done, I never wanted to smell PVC glue again (a heartfelt desire that, alas, was not granted me).

At last summer came, my friends returned, and I started working in earnest on the cabin. But something had changed. The carefree, relaxed atmosphere of the previous year had evaporated. I still swam in the river and partied with my friends, but I stopped hiking in the high country and declined to join the occasional pilgrimages to the hot springs on the coast.

I started working all the time.

I extended the thinning season, starting at the mouth of the valley and working my way north. I picked up odd carpentry jobs and spent a couple weeks cutting firewood to sell. And in between I kept building the house. It was slow, frustrating work. There was no electricity, so everything had to be done by hand or sometimes with a miniature and unreliable chainsaw. I probably spent more time pulling the cord on that damned thing than I did cutting with it. Plus, I didn't know what I was doing and learned far too often by the I-guess-you-don't-do-it-like-that method. But despite the obstacles, by the time the cold weather rolled around, with the dedicated help of several friends, I had the floor down, the walls raised, and the roof rafters up. But no windows or doors. No roof. And I was bone-tired, dispirited. Somehow I had gone from a happy-go-lucky lifestyle wherein I worked occasionally and had a lot of fun to a constant grind.

———

That year, when my friends went south for the winter, my girlfriend and I rented a place twenty miles away on Libby Creek. The house was huge but had no running water and no electricity. The windows lacked glass and were covered with two layers of clear plastic. The outhouse was fifty yards from the front door. But it was dirt cheap: thirty dollars per month. My girlfriend stuck with me through that winter, but when spring came, she decided she needed a vacation. We weren't breaking up, but she was going to California for a while. Looking back, it's not hard to imagine she was tired of woodstoves, outhouses, and kerosene lamps. She wanted a flush toilet, a hot shower, and a cold refrigerator.

And damned if I didn't want to go with her.

But I'd be double damned if I was going to quit before I finished the cabin — no matter how much I felt like giving up. I thinned my ass off that spring, running up the ladder and jumping off the fifth step all day long. By July, I got the roof on, and although there were still no windows or doors, the weather was warm, so I moved in. By September, just in time for the picking season, I got the windows in, built a kitchen counter, and plumbed in an old sink that I'd rescued from the dump. There was still a lot to do, but I called it done and threw a big housewarming party with lots of food and a keg of beer. Thirty people came, and two bald eagles circled the house for half an hour.

I was home.

In November, winter came with a vengeance, and I realized how poorly I had built. The metal schoolhouse windows I'd gotten cheap leaked like sieves. The logs weren't tight, the chinking between them inadequate. On cold nights when the woodstove was pumping, I could hear the wind whistling through the floorboards.

I stayed in the cabin all winter. On days when it wasn't too snowy, I pruned apple trees at a friend's orchard. I was the only one working there, and there were weeks when I didn't see another soul. By spring, my thoughts had dispersed, widened like a marshy delta. Emotions, ideas, and memories all combined into a viscous, slow-moving morass that made it hard to fish out linear strings of words when I did have occasion for conversation.

It was a remarkable time filled with stark contradictions. On the one hand, I was restless, dissatisfied, and uncertain what I was doing. But at the same time, I don't think I've ever felt quite so at home. It was intensely satisfying to live in the house I'd built, to go out on the deck in the morning and look down on the valley or lie in bed at night, listening to the creek babbling, the wind whispering in the aspen grove. It was quiet, it was beautiful, and it was mine. This was a big slice of real freedom. No matter what else happened, I would always have this beautiful place to call home.

**SAM:** During the time you were building and living in your cabin, I was ambivalent about your lifestyle. On the one hand, you worked like a demon during this period, and it put to rest any lingering fears I had about your work ethic. On the other hand, I was worried about where you were going with your life. I wasn't comfortable that you were twenty-two years old and still living hand to mouth. I wanted you to have direction and ambition. I wanted you to go to college.

By the time the cabin was complete and you were living there alone, I started hassling you to grow up, cut your hair, get a real job — with predictable results. Then one night, at the weekly meeting of a men's group I had been attending for ten years, I started talking about my anxiety. My friends laughed at me. "You mean he's supported himself with all kinds of jobs, grown much of his food, and built a cabin? What's the problem?"

One of my friends added, "He's doing something all of us have dreamed of."

I realized they were right. I relaxed, and even began vicariously enjoying your adventures.

**GIF:** While you were becoming comfortable with what I was doing, I was becoming increasingly restless. As spring pushed into summer, I found myself thinking more and more often: *You're twenty-two and your friends are* *graduating from college; what are you doing stuck here alone at the butt-end of nowhere?* I felt like life was passing me by. I could hear your voice echoing in the back of my mind: "So . . . are you planning to pick apples and dig ditches for the rest of your life?"

Well, was I?

It is strange. While it was happening, it seemed obvious that I was wasting my time. Yet in retrospect, that winter and the spring that followed comprised one of the most important periods of my life. In some ways, more than anything else I've done, it taught me who I was, what I was made of.

By early summer, though, I was lonely. None of my friends were planning to visit, and I missed my girlfriend. So one morning in June, without particularly having planned it, I threw my pack, skis, and an assortment of tools in the back of my beat-up truck and drove south.

That was thirty years ago, and I've only been back once. I hear from old friends that the deck has rotted off my cabin. A bear ripped the stovepipe off the roof, and a family of packrats has taken up tenancy. For many years, I expected to live there again — if not permanently, at least for many long, sun-drenched summers. There were so many things I planned to do, so many dreams built into the walls of that house. But at this point, I have to admit, it is unlikely I will return.

It never really struck me until I wrote this how much our relationship influenced my desire to build the cabin. And even more, how much the decision to finish it, when it would have been so much easier to quit, was bound up in our shared history. And even now, even though I haven't been back in over twenty years, that cabin still holds an important piece of my heart. Three of four times a year, I dream of it — big, colorful dreams that, when I wake, leave me filled with a strange mixture of optimism and nostalgia.

That house cost me my first love; it took two and a half years of the hardest work I've ever done to complete; and I only lived there for one year.

But I've never regretted it. Building the cabin transformed me. That one year, when I lived in the house I had built with my own hands, was perhaps the time in my life when I could say most confidently, "I am my own man. I mean *free*."

And that is not something one loses. Or forgets.

# chapter 24

# Work Makes the Man

Everyone has been made for some particular work, and the
desire for that work has been put in every heart.

— Rumi

**SAM:** From the distance of all we have learned in the last generation about
the hazards of being born male in this culture, my way of being a father
seems bizarre, if not mildly sadistic. But it isn't that simple. My identity as
a man was composed of a complex mixture of images, values, and myths
about work that I absorbed from my culture and notions about vocation I
got from the Calvinist tradition.

I was born in 1931, and my psyche was in large measure shaped by
the Great Depression. When unemployment was rampant and jobs scarce,
work became the great hope, the guiding star. Work was the secular god
(and demon), the path to the American Dream. The job, the paycheck, and
the capacity to take care of one's family were the taproots of meaning. To
be a man was to be employed. It was my "normal" American compulsion
to work and my obsession with my profession that made me unavailable
and controlling.

My program for turning you into man centered on work and roughly
followed the list of heroic virtues outlined in the Boy Scout laws (etched
into my mind from the legendary days when I was the youngest Eagle Scout
in Delaware). A Scout is (and I expected you to be) "trustworthy, loyal, helpful, friendly, courteous, kind, obedient, cheerful, thrifty, brave, clean, and
reverent," to which I added: truthful, tough, and a good worker. Needless
to say, you failed to live up to my impossible expectations. Following the
time-honored practice of the righteous earthly (and Heavenly) Father, I

was responsible for issuing commandments from on high, and you were responsible for obeying them. I stopped short of the biblical injunction to spare the rod and spoil the child, but I was critical, intimidating, and lacking in empathy.

My work life began when I went to Victory Farm Camp in 1944 at age fourteen. Since so many farm workers had been drafted, Boy Scouts were asked to cut asparagus on the sandy farms of lower Delaware. It was hot, backbreaking work with long hours and little pay (sixteen dollars for two weeks after room and board), but I rose (or bent) to the occasion and felt pride when one of the leaders said I was one of the best workers. In spite of the hard work, it felt like an adventure. We were excused from school, we lived in large tents, and we were treated to movies in the mess hall each evening, a treat otherwise denied me on religious grounds.

It took me years to realize that the "patriotic" farmers were getting rich on our contribution to the war effort.

At seventeen, on the hour I was supposed to attend my graduation ceremony, I drove west in my 1931 Model A Ford and ended up in Kansas, where I worked from sunup to sundown in the wheat fields, fueled by breakfasts of biscuits, eggs, ham, and pie; afternoon lemonade in the shade of the combine; and dinner (after a swim in the creek to wash the red dust from my body). Sleep, fathoms deeper than I had ever known.

The summer of '51 was hot, and jobs for college boys were scarce, so my brother and I felt lucky to get hired as trackmen (or "gandy dancers") on the Pennsylvania Railroad. Forty hours per week at one dollar twenty-five an hour and no overtime. During the week, we replaced broken railroad ties and raised track by pushing ballast underneath the ties with a jackhammer. On Friday afternoon, every man in the gang got a long bar and we pulled together to line the track so there wouldn't be any unwanted curves. The singer would start a chant, the men would all take it up, and we would pull together on the beat:

Captain, captain
Can't you see?
Lining bar
Is killing me

Seaboard Southern
L and N
Don't do nothing
But kill good men

Our crew, which was responsible for maintaining the track from Wilmington, Delaware to Marcus Hook, Pennsylvania, consisted of twelve black men and four white college boys. In the beginning, we honkeys were the butt of many jokes, all of which stressed how naïve and virginal we were. One day, when I was working with no shirt, J.D. Battle came over to me, pulled out a clump of his chest hair, and planted it on my bare torso.

"Hey, boy, you going to need a little more of this if you are going to get any free pussy."

Lampkin, a large black man who was the natural leader of the gang, chimed in, "Battle, them boys ain't ugly like you. They don't need no chest wig, and they don't have to pay for pussy."

Lampkin rapidly became guide and guru to the novices. He passed on the wisdom of the ages: "Boy, don't you start the day any faster than you intend to end it, 'cause this railroad is gon' be here when you dead and gone."

Over the summer, two separate events radically changed my brother's and my social status.

All the black men on the gang played the numbers, and, in a way I never understood, dreams were believed to predict the winning numbers. If, for instance, you dreamt about a pond with a duck on it, that might indicate that forty-five would be the winning number. In the mythology of the numbers game (as esoteric as the numerology of Pythagoras), it was also reckoned that the dreams of virgins (non-number players) were especially potent. At first Lawrence and I couldn't understand why, when we arrived at work, J.D. Battle would ask us what we had dreamt about the previous night. Weird. Then, one Monday morning, Battle swaggered in and announced he had won ninety-six dollars on a number he had divined from my brother's dream of a roan stallion. After that, Lawrence was considered the local equivalent of the Delphic oracle and was inundated each morning with requests for a word from the depths. Not since Freud had so many looked to the interpretation of dreams for revelation.

My ascendancy came about in a less mystical and substantially less honorable fashion. Like many manly men I pledged my allegiance to the NRA, and was fascinated by guns. I had managed to buy one rare LadySmith .22 pistol from a serious collector, and to sweeten the deal he threw in several "Saturday night specials" for which he had no use.

One afternoon while we were waiting for a train to pass, the subject of guns came up. One of the men whose house had been burgled said he would feel a lot safer if he owned a gun. I allowed that I could get him an inexpensive .32-caliber pistol. Within the week the deal was done, and several more besides. I don't remember how many I armed (not enough to get an award from Charlton Heston), but enough to wonder, at this late date, about the morality of my actions.

Working on the railroad was an important rite of passage. My initiation into the world of men came from the hard physical work I did well, and the pride I gained from working with other men to accomplish a task. My coming-of-age ritual on the railroad was being assigned to be J.D. Battle's partner in driving the spikes into the plates that held the rail in place. Once I picked up the hammer, I had to hit square and keep the pace. The first few times that I missed the spike, hit it crooked, or (God forbid) hit the shaft of the sledge, J.D. just smiled at me and said, "Don't worry; you'll get good at this pretty quick."

And I did. After that, I was just an ordinary young guy doing a man's job as well as anybody else.

I still feel a surge of recognition when I hear, "John Henry was a steel-driving man," and a small voice in my head answers, "so was I."

# chapter 25

# The Full Catastrophe

*For what is a man profited, if he shall gain the whole world,*
*and lose his own soul?*

— Matthew 16:26

**GIF:** When you first asked me for a story about my time in the software industry, I thought it would be a breeze to write. But whenever I tried to pull together an overarching theme or pick out particular stories that would capture the essence of those years, the threads diverged, snarled, and grew hopelessly tangled. This period of my life was one of profound ambivalence: an epoch of both great successes and heartrending failures.

So the story I want to tell is one that embraces two diametrically opposed, but intertwined, narratives.

The first is an almost archetypal American story of financial success. When I accepted a position at Los Alamos National Lab in 1990, I was thirty years old. Up until then I had worked a hodgepodge of temporary jobs, mostly outdoors, mostly physically demanding and mentally demeaning. I'd never made enough money to file income taxes. By the time I quit my job at a multinational corporation and walked away from a six-figure salary in 2001, I was financially independent, retired at forty.

The other side of the tale is darker, but no less archetypal. Those ten years hollowed me out. I started out fit, tan, boyish, and if not carefree (I've always been prone to existential angst), at least unburdened by responsibilities, unconcerned about status, and largely untouched by shame. I may not have had money, but I had freedom, independence, and self-respect. Nobody ran me.

By the time I had spent seven years in the biotech industry, I had a wife, two kids, and a mortgage. I was crippled by chronic back pain. I was working for a boss I despised, in a job I had come to hate; but I had too much invested, too much responsibility, too little courage to quit. In short, I sold my soul for prestige and money.

But let me start at the beginning. After four years at St. John's College, the vast New Mexico sky, unpopulated mountains, summer monsoons, and crisp winter days had worked their way beneath my skin. A liberal-arts education hadn't helped me decide what I wanted to do if I should ever grow up, but I wanted to stay in Santa Fe.

Through a strange set of circumstances, I ended up hearing about a position at Los Alamos National Lab as the manager of a small database that collected information about online resources for molecular biologists. At the time I knew little about molecular biology and less about computers. But I applied, interviewed, and was somehow offered the job.

The moral quandaries of my professional career began, in an insignificant but symbolic way, that very first day. As I was driving to work, I passed a carved wooden sign that read Welcome to Los Alamos, birthplace of the Atomic Age. Beneath the caption was a small rendering of what could only have been a mushroom cloud. A wave of moral disgust washed over me. What the hell was I doing, going to work at a weapons lab? But I fought back outrage and reminded myself that I would be working on a public database of DNA sequences — a good, humanitarian project. Still, it creeped me out.

Half an hour later, my new boss showed me to the cubicle that was to be my office for the next year. A dismal, fluorescently lit industrial space, it was so narrow that even with the chair pushed all the way back against the wall, there was barely room to slide between the seat and the desk. For a moment I balked; honestly, I almost quit before I even started. Except for a stint as a waiter, I'd never had an indoor job, and that cramped office epitomized everything I'd sworn I would never do. But it was only for a year, and I could always quit.

Or so I told myself.

I soon moved on from the small one-man project I'd been hired for, and got a job working on a big genomic database. I had a knack for software, and within a year, I was managing the programming group. Eventually, we spun the project out of the lab into a not-for-profit; and from there, into a for-profit startup where I was named Vice-President of Product Development. At each stage I was given additional responsibility, bigger raises, and eventually a boatload of stock options. And at each stage, that voice that told me I could always quit grew dimmer, and I felt more trapped.

Finally, seven years and a lot of hard miles after I had first sat in that dismal cubicle, our for-profit company was bought by a big multinational corporation and my worthless stock options in the startup were converted to real stock in the new company, which was listed on the NY Stock Exchange. I had managed to live the Silicon Valley dream without leaving Santa Fe.

During the years between spinning the project out of the lab and our startup being bought, my ambivalence toward my career grew so pronounced that I often felt like two different people.

In one world, I was having the time of my life. At my peak, I was managing three major software projects and was involved in the design of all of them. The technical work was all consuming. I was leading a group of fifty bright people and we were building huge, complicated database systems to deal with an unprecedented deluge of genomic data. And we were close. More than coworkers, more even than friends, our development group was knit together by long hours, shared sacrifices, the risks of failure, the rewards of success. I loved writing serious software; it was the single most obsessively compelling thing I'd ever done. I still look back on this period of my life with nostalgia and more than a little longing.

But even as the technical challenges grew more exciting and the dream of wealth became a tactile possibility, the business realities grew proportionately uglier. With the new startup, I had a new boss, whom I grew to despise. After the Challenge Discovery trip, when I was fourteen, I'd promised myself I would never let anyone push me around again. But my new boss treated me with smug, superior contempt. He belittled me and forced me to perform senseless, distasteful tasks just to assert his power. And I took it. I smiled and kissed his ass when I wanted nothing more than to spit in his face, and in so doing I broke the pact I had made with myself.

One day when my boss was being particularly horrible, I lost my temper and stormed out of his office, slamming the door so hard that all the windows on the second floor shook. I went to my office, called my wife Karin, and told her what had happened. She was outraged, and told me if I wanted to quit I should march right back in and tell my boss to shove it. She didn't care if we had to cut back or even if we had to move to California. Karin advised me to do whatever I wanted and let the chips fall where they may.

I think if she'd said, "It's a really good job, honey," or "Think hard. What will we do if you quit?" it would have broken me. But instead, her staunch, indignant, unqualified support gave me the strength to go on. I will always love her for that.

So in the end I stayed. I had a mortgage to pay and a family to support. Also, by this time I was making a six-figure salary and had enough stock options that if the company were ever bought, I could have what my boss called "fuck-you money." This, he explained to me in condescending tones, meant I'd be rich enough to say "fuck you" to anyone I wanted. (Guess who was going to be first on my list?)

Should I have walked away from all that? And even if I'd wanted to quit, I felt responsible for my employees. I couldn't let them down. I told myself it was compromise, not betrayal; I had gone too far to turn back, and it would all be worth it in the end.

So I knuckled under and swallowed my pride. I worked longer hours and started traveling — at first just occasionally, then a couple times a month, and eventually as many as one hundred days per year. I gave up birthdays and anniversaries. I worked nights and weekends. My position at work became untenable. Management thought I was a techno-geek who didn't understand the realities of business, while the developers viewed me as a management stoolie. There was no way to reconcile those two worlds, and I had to force compromises that left everyone (including me) feeling like I'd sold them out. At a certain point, there was no path I could walk with integrity. Anything I did would betray someone.

**SAM:** After you started working at the lab, neither one of us thought you would last at a desk job. You'd done well in college, but still I was amazed at your meteoric rise in the bioinformatics business, especially since you knew nothing about either computers or biology. As your career progressed, I was proud of you and delighted when you started making a lot of money. I bragged shamelessly about you to my friends.

But, at the same time, I wasn't comfortable with your transformation from hippy to businessman, and I worried about the toll it was taking. You were less spontaneous, more stressed out, consumed by your profession — as I had been. I knew your chronic back pain was a sign that you could not bear the weight of what you were doing.

You talked to me during this period about your moral ambivalence toward your job. But it wasn't until I read this story that I realized how conflicted you were. I wonder now: When in your career did you realize that what you were doing was morally wrong?

**GIF:** There was no single Faustian moment when the Devil appeared and offered me my heart's desire in exchange for my soul. It happened so gradually, one small piece at a time, that I hardly noticed. There was no one concession that didn't seem reasonable at the time. If you throw a frog into a pan of hot water, it will jump right out. But if you put it in cool water and slowly raise the temperature, it will sit there until it cooks.

So when should I have jumped? That first day, when I'd seen the depiction of a mushroom cloud on the sign by Los Alamos? When I'd first been offered a managerial position? When my boss started pushing me around?

And if I had quit, what kind of father and husband would I have become? What would I have done instead?

I don't know. But I do remember when I could no longer deny that I'd ended up in hot water.

It was the fall of 1997. I was in the midst of a ten-day, twelve-city sales tour of the industrial pits of Northern Europe when I found myself walking up to the main headquarters of BASF in Ludwigshafen, Germany. On this particular dreary, overcast morning, I was nauseated from little sleep and bad hotel food. I hadn't seen the sun in five days, and I'd also managed while shaving to slice open a big mole on my right cheek that wouldn't stop bleeding. But I was dressed for success: blue pinstripe suit, pressed white shirt, conservative tie, and shiny wingtips. The black leather briefcase in my hand was pregnant with my laptop, presentation materials, white papers for the clients, and painkillers for my back. My heart was filled with an even heavier weight: equal parts excitement, self-importance, and existential loathing.

And the scenery didn't help. The town of Ludwigshafen was built around BASF, a monstrous pharmaceutical and chemical company. Factories stretched for four miles along both sides of the Rhine; the large, slow river ran a cool blue, flowing into the complex before being ejected a murky, toxic brown on the other side. With its tall stacks belching black smoke or tipped with flame, and massive networks of pipes and gigantic, rounded tanks at the tops of towers, the landscape resembled nothing less than an archetypal, Daliesque tableau of industrial hell.

Then, as I was making my way up the steps to an impressive stone edifice with BASF embossed over the portal, for just a moment, the sick irony of the situation broke over me like a malevolent wave.

Not that long ago I had been living on the farm in Washington, growing organic vegetables, hiking in the back country, smoking pot and taking acid, swimming in the river, often wearing nothing for days but a ragged pair of shorts and a filthy, fluorescent-yellow baseball cap with CAT DIESEL POWER inscribed on the front.

And now, here I was in a damned business suit, with a doubly dammed tie choking the life out of me, preparing to suck up to a bunch of soulless suits inside this horrible building in this truly godforsaken place. It struck me that the moral aesthetics of my current situation had passed beyond questionable and entered unambiguously into the realm of depravity. That massive, stinking blot of corruption on the earth, the metallic smell of pollution in the air, the toxic effluent that I could see pouring into the river, had transported me far beyond any hope of self-justification; it stripped me of even the pretense of denial.

I would like to say I tore off my tie, threw my laptop in the Rhine, and ran off into the sunset, determined to change my life for the better. After all, this was an *epiphany*. The very word is rich with connotations of immediacy, of sudden insight, irrevocable change. But in fact, other than an added leaden feeling of hopelessness, or perhaps an incremental lump of nausea as I shrugged off the moment and started up the steps to my meeting, I'm not sure I even knew what had happened.

There have been several turning points in my life like this: huge moments where something fundamental broke, or changed, or grew inside of me, and I didn't know what it meant until much later. It took more than three years (and a lot of luck and pain and hard work and courage and cowardice) for the change that had taken root in my heart that grey, morally empty morning in Ludwigshafen to grow and eventually flower into a new life.

# chapter 26

# Freelancing

Doubt everything. Find your own light.

— The Buddha

**SAM:** No sooner had I resigned from a secure, tenured professorship than I was caught in a whirlwind that set the tone of my professional life for the next forty years. When the editor of *Psychology Today*, T. George Harris, invited me to write for the magazine, I began a decade-long period during which I established myself as chronicler of the emerging New Age movement. I published dozens of interviews with leading luminaries from the wide and woolly range of the human-potential movement.

Two years into my freelance career, I decided to interview Carlos Castaneda, the creator of Don Juan Matus — the mythic darling of the counterculture. At first, my peers and most of the editors at the magazine were skeptical. They all thought that the interview would tarnish *Psychology Today*'s credibility, but I felt that the interest in Castaneda was widespread. So, despite their dire warnings, I invoked the Keen Way and pushed ahead. The interview was wildly successful, far more than even I had hoped, and ended up being one of the most widely quoted articles of the year.

From this point forward, I was swept up by the current of the times, and my new career took off. The phone calls came rolling in. I was swamped with requests for interviews and articles. Without quite intending it, I became an interpreter of the New Age movement.

One of the high points of this era was when Michael Murphy of Esalen and I put on a large conference on "Spiritual and Therapeutic Tyranny."

At the time, the New Age movement was a hodgepodge of loose spirituality — gurus who held themselves up as enlightened, and therapies whose claims to healing were unsubstantiated. What started as new philosophies often ended as cults of personality. Since I had perfected the role of devil's advocate while teaching in the seminary, it was a natural extension to apply these talents to the new psychologies. The field needed critique.

The conference took place at the Academy of Sciences in the Presidio in San Francisco and was well attended. Five hundred people packed the auditorium, many of whom where graduates of New Age programs like EST, psychosynthesis, and Arica or were disciples of the gurus and "enlightened beings" who were participating in the conference. All the various luminaries were arrayed in a predatory semicircle behind me on stage when I delivered the keynote address on "The Tyranny Game" in which I hinted that many of them might be practitioners of spiritual tyranny. I slayed them with a smile, laying bare the ways cults are formed, exposing the fuzzy thinking of many of the new therapies, and mocking the shallow nature of the cult of personality.

It was quite a scene.

After my talk, many of the gurus told me that while my criticisms might apply to others, in their cases my accusations were baseless and offensive. The leaders of psychosynthesis, which by now had morphed into a tightly controlled cult, even forbade their members to speak to me.

I have to confess I took perverse pleasure in being a spiritual hit man. But even more important than public acclaim was the effect this incident had on my psyche. It was at this moment that I realized I had finally lain the ghost of my mother to rest. In the face of her taboo (*Thou shall not doubt*), I affirmed as a philosopher that the maxim I was committed to follow was Descartes' "Cogito ergo sum": *I think (or doubt); therefore, I am.* And far from facing punishment or approbation, I even got paid for it.

I had fulfilled my promise to myself.

———

The greatest satisfactions of my career came from the knowledge that my inner-directed quests were helpful to others. By sharing my struggles with orthodox Christianity in *To a Dancing God* and with manhood in *Fire in the Belly*, I articulated experiences many people shared but had been unable to put into words. Without intending to, I became a "permissionary" by encouraging those who felt imprisoned in oft-told myths to explore their stories. I will never forget the man who came up to me after a lecture and said, with tears in his eyes, "Thank you, thank you. You are my words. You have told my life story."

**GIF:** While this account of your freelance career is compelling, it seems one-sided. It doesn't deal with the dichotomy between your professional and personal lives.

One of my most intimate experiences of you (before we began writing this book) came on a cool fall evening years ago as I sat in a darkened auditorium at the College of Santa Fe with five hundred strangers, listening to your lecture on the Faces of the Enemy.

Earlier in the evening, we had gone to dinner at your favorite Italian restaurant, and I remember you seemed distracted — tense, jumpy. You told three or four jokes, but your timing was off; they weren't funny.

But an hour later, when the lights dimmed and you strode onto the stage, a man appeared whom I hardly felt I knew. With no props other than a metal folding chair and a clicker to change the slides, you kept that audience (and me) riveted to their seats. But it wasn't just the content of the lecture. It was you. Everything about you seemed different. Your face was unlined and open, your voice rich and full, your body fluid with an unfamiliar ease.

On that stage, in front of all those people, you radiated charisma and a sense of intimacy that made each and every person feel you were talking to them alone. For two hours, you addressed us without distraction, mesmerizing us with every iota of your attention. You were present in a way I had never seen.

Well, *almost* never. As I sat in that dark auditorium watching you with a bizarre mixture of emotions — pride, wonder, dismay — a recurring experience, poignantly typical of our relationship, came to mind. We'd be having lunch in a restaurant, often ill at ease, searching for some way to connect, and a stranger would approach. "You're Sam Keen," he would invariably start. "I took your workshop at . . . " or "I heard you speak in . . . " or "I've read your books." Then you would invite him to sit, rewarding your fan with that same full-on attention, answering questions with a level of intimacy and thoughtful kindness that drove me into insane fits of jealousy.

These encounters made me deeply uncomfortable, and I always told myself the reason was that you were being a phony. This wasn't the real you — and who would know better than I? But it was that night at the College of Santa Fe that, in a very true sense, I realized that this *was* the real you. It was I, not your fans, who hadn't really seen you.

All these years.

During that lecture, I caught a glimpse of the father I had always wanted.

**SAM:** For many years, I paid far more attention to career than family. That is, at least in part, why I was professionally successful. But I paid a heavy price. I was often lonely, and the focus on career cost me the intimacy I longed for with the ones I loved the most — my family.

But the other side of that coin is that for many years the family didn't treat me well. It was ironic. On the road, I was a star; my work was appreciated. I was a prince. But coming home, I became a frog. I was constantly criticized, and I never felt appreciated.

In retrospect, it's easy to see the self-reinforcing nature of this cycle. Professionally, I became more and more comfortable. I felt most alive when I was working. At home, I became more and more defended, and after a time, of course you didn't admire me — I was too withdrawn to let my real self shine through.

By temperament, I am introverted. I am most comfortable when I am engaged in the life of the mind. More than anything, I am moved by eros for ideas. Philosophy is not an occupation; it is a passion. One effect of this is that I sometimes ignore the people in my immediate environment. My loved ones have often complained that I don't pay attention. But that's not really the problem. I am paying attention. It's just to something else. I'm off somewhere romancing a strange idea. The very same love of ideas that made me professionally successful also makes me occasionally unavailable — at least to others. This is my greatest strength and my most difficult flaw. And it is not something I could change, even if I wanted to.

Another aspect of this issue is simply the commitment it takes for a man to have a successful career in our culture. After your time in the bio-tech industry, I'm sure you know this exceedingly well.

So I wonder about the tradeoffs.

Could I have succeeded in my career if I had focused more on my family? Even if I had wanted to, could I have done so without killing my passion? Can a modern man fully dedicate himself to his career without, like Abraham, sacrificing his firstborn?

# chapter 27

# Power, Intimacy, and the Composting Toilet

Everyone talks about leaving a better world for our children;
how about leaving better children for our world?

— Anonymous

**GIF:** When my son, Jasper, was nine, we bought a farm on the Big Island of Hawaii — eleven acres, three small houses, no electricity, every variety of fruit you could imagine, and twenty years of neglect. We arrived late on a Tuesday afternoon in December after a sixteen-hour plane ride with four hundred pounds of luggage, a rented Jeep to carry us up the rough lava driveway, and a heavy burden of dreams. I had spent only three hours on the property the previous September, and neither Karin nor the kids had ever seen it.

When we got there, the house was a disaster. Instead of preparing for our arrival, as we'd agreed, the previous owner had looted the place. She had taken the propane tanks so we couldn't run the fridge; most of the solar panels were gone, so we had virtually no electricity. There were dirty dishes in the sink, boxes of castoff possessions cluttering the floor, piles of garbage everywhere. And roaches.

The verdict is still out on whether buying that place was the smartest thing I've ever done or the dumbest. Or maybe both. But that first year, moving from a large, comfortable house in Santa Fe with all the modern conveniences most Americans take for granted (like electricity) to a three-hundred-square-foot, off-grid shack in the wilds of Hawaii was indeed a struggle.

On the second day, Karin and I sat down with the kids and told them that we'd landed in a tight spot (which they'd already figured out), and that if we were going to make it work, we really needed their help. The results were nothing short of miraculous. At the time Jasper was nine and Caitlin twelve, but they did the dishes every night and kept their stuff picked up. They cleaned and weeded the yard. They worked side by side with Karin and me, in most cases without being asked.

What was it about this situation that made the children work so cheerfully?

It took a while to realize that for the first time in their lives, the children's labor was necessary. Throughout human evolution, children's work had been integral to the survival of the family. But for most contemporary, middle-class American families — and ours had previously been no exception — children were fundamentally useless, parasites on the body politic of the family. There was an atavistic rightness to those weeks we spent working together that I still feel down to my bones. And the kids felt it too — they wanted to help because we needed them, and they knew it.

But the most magical part of this process was how, through some alchemy that was both obvious and mysterious, the positive behaviors fed on themselves. The more the kids helped, the more approval they received. The more approval they got, the harder they worked. Karin and I became inordinately proud of the children, which in turn made them even more eager to help — not because they felt guilty or obligated, but because they felt loved and admired.

The next year, when we returned to Hawaii, I bought and installed a composting toilet in the main house. It was, perhaps, the single stupidest thing I've done in the last decade — and there have been some remarkable contenders for that dubious honor. Like so many wretched mistakes, all I can say now is that it seemed like a good idea at the time.

It was the top-of-the-line, six-adults-full-time, best-reviewed composting toilet on the market: three grand with shipping. The first fingers of trepidation started massaging my spine when it came out of the box. It just didn't seem right. Five feet long and about three high, it resembled nothing more than a fat, short coffin with two holes in the top — one for the vent stack and one for the poo. Made of cheap, flimsy, white plastic with a skinny, black crank handle on the side, it weighed about twenty pounds and looked as if it should have cost more like three hundred than three thousand.

It took two days, every curse word I knew, and a few I invented along the way to get the damn thing installed. And then the fun started. It never worked right. The little twelve-volt fan that pushed the stink up the vent gave out twice, leaving the house smelling like a New York subway for two weeks while a new one was being shipped from Canada. Twice a week I had to go under the house, open the little access hatch (I don't suppose I have to describe to what the hatch gave access), add a special bulking agent (which cost a bundle and could only be bought from the maker of the toilet), and crank the big bin around a dozen times.

In theory, ninety-five percent of the organic matter in the toilet tank (read shit) was supposed to decompose aerobically and exit the vent stack as vapor, leaving behind a light, odorless compost perfect for gardens. But — as the car commercials say — your mileage may vary.

To make a long story short, about a year after installing it, we returned to the farm after an absence, and the damn toilet, instead of composting, was filling up. I dutifully went through the troubleshooting guide, bought new enzymes, added more bulking agent, and cranked the bin around and around until I thought my arm would fall off.

But all to no avail.

Then late one Friday afternoon, as I was turning the putrid not-compost, and trying to convince myself that the contents weren't fouler and the bin fuller than they had been a week ago, the access hatch burst open mid-turn and disgorged twenty gallons of vile, foul-smelling sludge onto the ground under the house.

It wasn't thirty seconds before Karin was out on the lanai calling down to me, "Oh my God, what is that stench?"

I changed into my oldest clothes, armed myself with a respirator, latex gloves, several five-gallon buckets, a shovel, and copious quantities of bleach, then crawled back under the house. In fifteen years as a landlord, I've cleaned up a lot of revolting messes, more of them dealing with clogged pipes and sewage than I care to recall. But this was, hands down, the dirtiest, most nauseating, just plain nastiest job I've ever done. Even with a respirator cinched tight, the smell was overpowering, and the urge to vomit only slightly less.

So there I was under the house, scooping filth into buckets with my hands, swearing and gagging and generally cursing myself for being an idiot. About the third time I crawled out with a loaded bucket, I looked up, and there was Jasper. He'd changed into a ragged pair of jeans; his toes were sticking out of the ends of an old, too-small pair of tennis shoes; he had a red bandanna tied across his nose and mouth, and a pair of leather work gloves on his hands. He was holding a bucket. On his face was an expression of grim determination mixed with absolute loathing. He was eleven years old.

"How can I help?" he asked.

The sun was beginning to set, the odor still permeating the house, and even in the depth of my disgust, I remember stopping in my tracks and looking at him in wonder. But no matter how much I would have liked some help, I didn't want to subject him to this.

"You really need a respirator," I told him after a moment. "And there's only one. But thanks anyhow."

Eventually I got the crap cleaned up. Then Karin, Jasper, and I dragged the tank from under the house and pulled it as far into the jungle as we could — it weighed over five hundred pounds. I was out there at five thirty the next morning digging a sewer line to the old cesspool. After a long trip to the Home Depot in Kona and an even longer day, the new, conventional toilet was installed and flushing by dark.

Then I burned the clothes and shoes I'd used for the job.

The whole episode was disgusting, expensive, and embarrassing. But I wouldn't trade it for the world. That image of Jasper, standing in the fading evening light, his mouth covered by a bandanna, his face etched with disgust and pride, is burnt into my heart. I will never forget it.

At that moment, some basic fear about my ability to father a son melted like butter in the summer sun, and I knew I had done something very right. I knew I could count on my son's help, but even more importantly, I was assured of his affection. Because it was neither guilt nor fear nor a Calvinist sense of responsibility that brought him to my aid that night, but rather love.

Needless to say, when I was eleven, a team of mules couldn't have dragged me out to help you clean up raw sewage. But Jasper offered his help without being asked.

Why? What was the difference?

The culture around fatherhood has changed dramatically in the last half-century. When I was young, the accepted social wisdom was that children, like milk, were easily spoiled. The underlying parenting myth of the times closely followed the Christian doctrine of original sin. Without guidance, you assumed, I would be slothful, disinclined toward work, disinterested in education. It was your responsibility — *nay*, your sacred duty — to shape me up, make me work, teach me to obey and to be respectful. In short, to turn me into a Man.

And given my behavior, it must have seemed a long, hard row to hoe.

But Karin and I took the opposite approach. As much as we were able, we raised Jasper and Caitlin according to the doctrine of original perfection. We tried to assume they were perfect and our job, as parents, was to screw them up as little as possible, while still preventing them from putting knives in outlets or running headlong into traffic — activities Jasper was all too eager to attempt when young.

I wish I could say that we chose this philosophy through clear-eyed consideration, but I think it was as much a response to our history as any other factor. Just as you were determined not to live in your father's shadow, we refused to raise our son in yours.

One, perhaps counterintuitive, result of this philosophy was, since I didn't try to force Jasper to work, whenever I was laboring he wanted to help. After leaving the corporate life, I was blessed with a lot of time around the family, and, especially in Hawaii, I did a lot of manual work: electrical, plumbing, ditch-digging, construction. Jasper was often there, and for those first years, his "assistance" generally meant it took me three times longer to accomplish anything. I remember you used to say to me, "If things don't start going better, I'm going to have to ask you to stop helping." That bon mot did occur to me more than once with Jasper; but whenever possible, I tried to take the extra time to let him "help." Now he's a teenager (and taller than me), and this investment has paid off in spades. He's strong, willing, and competent. He often volunteers his help without being asked. In virtually any situation, having him with me makes it easier and, best of all, more fun.

In the light of the story of Jasper and the composting toilet, it seems odd that the true nature of our conflicts eluded me for so many years. Our struggles — from the Egg, all the way through to our fight at Pasqual's — were not actually about work. They were about power. We didn't fight because I didn't know how to work, or even because I didn't want to. We fought because you were trying to coerce me to do things I didn't want to do.

What I discovered with Jasper is that there is an inverse relationship between intimacy and power. If I had tried to force him to work, he and I would have become adversaries, as you and I had. But by working together, we became friends — shared work became shared intimacy. I think this is perhaps the most important thing I have learned as a parent: There is nothing more corrosive to intimacy than the exercise of power, and nothing more conducive to friendship between parents and children than mutual respect.

Looking back, I can't help thinking how easy it would have been to change the power dynamic that alienated us from each other, if only we could have seen it for what it was. What I most wanted was to be with you, to be close to you. And I suspect you would have given anything to have a loving, cooperative son. How I wish it could have been that way for us.

# PART IV
# HOMECOMING

The hero may well come up against a "father figure" who must be beaten, persuaded, or whose approval must be achieved in some way. Ultimately, by whatever means, the difficult relationship between the two must be reconciled.

— Joseph Campbell

# chapter 28

# Raising the Roof

A free spirit needs a dwelling.

— Sandor McNab

**SAM:** By my midcentury mark, I'd lived in a dozen states and in more houses than I could count. I had become a man perpetually on the way — restless and rootless, never at home.

The urge to settle came on gradually, and at first I resisted. It felt like betraying the dreams of youth and settling for the comforts of age. All of this changed when I first drove into the small town of Sonoma and had a strange feeling of déjà vu, a sense of familiarity. When I got home, I phoned a longtime resident of Sonoma and asked if she knew of any land for sale.

"I know a Benedictine monk who owns 120 acres in the hills, and he has to sell half of his property to complete his hermitage."

"Say no more. I'll be there tomorrow morning."

Coming through the gate into Sky Farm felt like entering Shangri-La. The small valley embraced by high hills was as isolated from the town of Sonoma as if it were in the middle of Wyoming. It was hilly and wild, with no electricity, telephone, or road. There were no bridges over the two creeks and no visible neighbors except for wild turkeys, coyotes, and bobcats. The land had not been inhabited for decades and had returned to a disheveled, pristine condition. I knew immediately it was a place to settle.

I agreed on a price for Sky Farm with Father Dunstan, the Benedictine monk who owned the land. My plan was to relocate there from Muir Beach, where the damp, the mold, and the foggy winters had become unbearable. I began wrestling with the county bureaucracies to get permission to split the parcel and build the house I had constructed in my imagination. Almost a year later, the bureaucracy moved through its petty paces, and I became the overwhelmed owner of a farm three miles from downtown Sonoma — sixty idyllic acres covered with grassy meadows, live oak, and bay trees.

After waiting an inordinate time for building permits, I decided I would start to build without official permission. I reasoned: What was the chance that log-rolling, indecisive, cover-your-ass-with-paper county officials were going to say, "Tear it down"? Now all I needed was somebody who knew how to build a house.

My son?

**GIF:** "I'm sorry, Dad," I remember saying into the phone, "but I don't think I can come out there for four months. I've got a lot going on right now."

This wasn't strictly true, but the thought of leaving New Mexico and going to work for you in California seemed fraught with peril. There was a long pause, soft static stretching taut over the phone line, and I thought for a moment you might have hung up.

"Gif, there's no one else I can ask," you said. "I really need your help, son."

There was something in your voice that caught my attention, an unfamiliar tone that called to me. And the request itself was unprecedented. I'd never heard you ask anyone for help before — especially not me. An even longer silence ensued. While you waited, I tried to wrap my head around the concept that you were in a tight spot and were reaching out to me.

"Okay," I said. "I'll fly out next week."

**SAM:** I waited impatiently, aware I had a lot of ambivalence about your coming. Would we be able to work together without conflict? Would old animosities emerge in new forms now that our roles were being reversed — you becoming the foreman, and me the laborer?

———

**GIF:** A few days later, I found myself standing by a foundation and a partially constructed floor on a frosty November morning with a tool belt strapped around my waist and a confused expression on my face. The tools were because I was supposed to be helping build your new house, and the confusion stemmed from the fact that someone had put about a quarter of the floor on so crookedly that the edges of the plywood didn't come close to lining up with the floor joists. It would have to be torn up and redone.

You'd hired a contractor who we nicknamed the "Mallard," and at first, I couldn't figure out why you thought you needed me. I'd worked on and off as a carpenter for seven years and was a competent framer, but I soon realized that, although the Mallard was only a moderately skilled builder, he was a prodigious bullshit artist — and not overburdened with integrity. Even that first day, as I was swearing and ripping up plywood, he took off for town, ostensibly to pick up materials, and didn't return for the rest of the day. Nor did it take long to discover that he was running two other jobs (a fact he failed to disclose to you) and that he was billing you for forty hours a week when he often spent less than thirty on the site and even fewer actually working.

The other member of the crew was the Mallard's son-in-law, an unsavory specimen named Ben. As it turned out, he'd recently been fired from his job as an accountant at a soft-drink company. He was in his mid-thirties, fat, badly out of shape, and had zero experience working construction. But what he lacked in aptitude, he more than made up for with a complete lack of enthusiasm and an undetectable work ethic. He bitched, he whined, he malingered. I found him intolerable.

One day about three weeks after I arrived, the clueless moron walked right into a wall brace and smacked his forehead. After recovering for half an hour (instead of thirty seconds), he said, "It's a good thing I wasn't running when I hit that thing."

To which I replied, "What are the chances of that?"

That about summed up our relationship.

Suffice it to say that on that first day, as I tore up the new floor and chiseled the dried glue off the joists while Ben sat on his ass and whined, I was already beginning to see why you wanted help.

**SAM:** Within the next couple of weeks the walls were framed — a frail castle of sticks giving the first hint of the shape to come — and the big day came for raising the roof beams. Inevitably, the project assumed the character of a mythic event — like an old-fashioned barn-raising. The two massive glulam beams that were to support the roof were each thirty-two feet long, twenty-one inches tall, five inches wide, and so heavy we needed a crew of ten to wrestle them sixteen feet in the air into the slots in the walls that had been framed to hold them.

Six friends and neighbors swelled our crew to ten, not counting the Mallard and the son-in-law in whom we were not well pleased. Through one long day, you and I guided the beams precariously upward until they fit snuggly into their predestined places. By nightfall the job was done, and we broke out the beer to celebrate.

Later, you reminded me that we could have rented a crane that would have safely lifted the ridge beams into place in ten minutes or so. You suspected (then and now) that I wanted the heroic challenge of lifting those damned things by hand. True — I was happy we did it the old way because there is nothing like a house-raising to bring a community together.

**GIF:** I think at first it was hard for you to trust me. After all, our interactions around work had never been easy, and you'd never seen me in action as an adult. But that began to change pretty fast. When you showed me the Mallard's hours for that first week, I knew he was ripping you off. After that, I kept his timesheet and insisted that Ben (the least skilled and lowest paid), not he, make trips to town for materials.

And I worked my ass off, getting there before seven and staying until five thirty, so despite the obstacles we made decent progress. (Even though there was a three-man crew, it seemed I did three quarters of the framing.)

You realized quickly that I knew what I was doing. And so, once we got the walls framed and the roof beams raised, on a warm, joyful day you fired the Mallard. He packed up, took Ben with him, and I was suddenly the foreman.

**SAM:** As the weeks went on, our roles became clear, and we worked together not only without conflict but with growing appreciation. My most important job as contractor made use of my skills as a bargain hunter and involved purchasing the necessary materials, having them on the jobsite, and getting the subcontractors who were doing the plumbing and wiring to show up when we needed them. A day early and we weren't ready; a day late and we had to tread water.

When my higher skills as manager of materials, paymaster, and interface with the Sonoma County inspectors were not in demand, I was a carpenter's apprentice charged with nailing off vast reams of flooring, siding, and roofing — but was not trusted to tackle any job that required exact measurements or neat joints. In addition, I was the cleanup man. I couldn't escape the feeling that you took fiendish delight at the end of each day when you instructed me to clean the worksite before morning. I think we both appreciated the irony of the situation, and I took special care to do a good job with no complaints; you took care not to criticize my performance. How transformational was that!

**GIF:** After the Mallard flew south, I hired a couple of drug-addicted carpenters who were friends of friends of mine, and when they managed to show up, they actually did a decent job. So the house continued to grow, and over the next weeks something happened that was little short of miraculous. You and I got along great. We didn't argue. We didn't fight. We didn't even disagree much. I don't remember feeling resentful, angry, sarcastic, or annoyed, not even once. This was especially remarkable because we were intertwined in a strange and potentially explosive set of complex power / authority relationships.

On one hand, I was the foreman, and you often worked as a laborer. This meant that not only did I tell you what to do, but as the least skilled worker, you got a lot of the crappy jobs. You didn't even complain (well — not much) when I had you standing on a fifteen-foot scaffold for a week working over your head, sanding and staining all the ceiling beams.

On the other side of the coin, you were the owner, banker, and boss. You signed the checks and were the final authority on design decisions. There were two narrow windows running alongside the main upright beam in the living room, and at one point you asked me to change their dimensions at least three, maybe four times, on each occasion making them longer. This meant that each time I had to rip out the window framing and do it again — just the kind of decision that usually generates derision among a crew.

But somehow I didn't mind at all. Really.

Looking back, I still marvel at how well we worked together, how much fun we had, and how easy it was between us. We fought regularly and sometimes bitterly prior to building that house, and in the decade after, while I was pursuing a career and raising a family, our old conflicts continued to simmer just below the surface. But for those magical months, all the old patterns were transcended. For that brief season we fell into grace, simply enjoyed each other's company, and lost ourselves in the beauty of shared work — together as father and son.

**SAM:** One of my most vivid memories of building together was of the day we worked frantically to finish nailing down the two-by-six, tongue-in-groove ceiling, then rushed to cover the whole thing with tarpaper to protect it from an approaching storm. During the previous weeks we had enjoyed ideal weather, but now high winds and dark clouds were moving in. The forecast was for heavy rains, and it was clear the storm would be on us before the end of the afternoon. As the winds gathered strength, the tarpaper threatened to become one long kite.

For hours we were locked into a rhythm, in perfect sync, working as fast as we could, sweat flowing, one purpose with four hands. Unroll a yard, staple it down, unroll another yard, staple that down, et cetera. We moved together like two dancers executing an intricately choreographed ballet. There was something theatrical about it — two small actors on a bare stage surrounded by thunderheads, suggestive of Wagner's *Ride of the Valkyries*. At one moment I looked over at you and was overwhelmed by feelings of gratitude and pride. You were perfect; our dance was perfect. I still feel the primal perfection of that day. We were so closely bonded — father and son — in what was a ritual of initiation for us both.

Clearly, the cosmic stage manager was alert, because we had no sooner finished nailing the last of the tarpaper than the rain began, at first gentle and then a downpour accompanied by lightning and thunder. We retreated to the interior of the house and sat quietly for a long time, dry, listening to the sound of rain on the new roof.

Now, a quarter of a century later when the wind and torrential rains sweep down the valley like a wild banshee, the house creaks a little like a ship under sail, and I sit confidently in my living room remembering how many storms we have weathered, knowing that what we built together was built to last. Daily, as I inhabit this consecrated house, I feel an abiding sense of gratitude to you. What you helped me do was not merely construct a house, but create a world that encompassed the height and depth of my being. Because you are forever an integral part of my life — blood of my blood, bone of my bone — you were the only one who could help me perform the archetypal act by which the prodigal father could come home.

Thank you, my son.

# chapter 29

# Statute of Limitation

To err is human, to forgive, divine.

— Alexander Pope

**SAM:** It happened so rapidly; we were changed in an instant.

It started when my wife, Patricia, and I went to Iran on a citizen's diplomacy mission to talk with Iranian cartoonists about the ways political art dehumanizes the enemy. After a preliminary meeting at the House of Cartoons, we agreed to have an extended dialogue the following weekend. But when we arrived, we were informed by our governmental handlers that the cartoonists were out of town. All of them? Yes, all of them.

As it happened, a Muslim cleric who was also a professor of law at the university was free for lunch. We met at a charming open-air café and fell into conversation for a couple of hours. When it was time to leave, I failed to notice my leg had fallen asleep. The moment I put weight on it, it buckled, and I fell forward, first striking my head on the iron railing of the eating platform, then flipping over it, headfirst to the stone floor four feet below. I heard a sickening *thunk*, like an overripe cantaloupe hitting the ground and knew I was in trouble. The next thing I remember, I was curled on the floor wiping blood from my eyes. A cosmetic surgeon who had been having lunch at an adjacent table located the nearest emergency room, and within the hour I had received a CAT scan, my wound was sutured, my head was wrapped in a full-gauze turban, and I was pronounced travel-worthy.

Except for looking like a zombie and having a dull headache, everything seemed normal when we arrived home. But three weeks later when I resumed trapeze practice, I noticed that every time I fell into the net, I felt an ache on the left side of my head. At Patricia's insistence I went to the doctor, and she decided to do another CAT scan. Half an hour later, she returned with a large photographic negative of my brain that looked like storm clouds gathering over Kansas. "You have a sizable subdural hematoma," she announced. This sounded ominous, but I was relieved when she said she was going to give me steroids and see if the hematoma would dissolve. I went home clutching my medicine bottles and waited to be pronounced healed.

Two weeks later, I returned for a checkup, and there was little change. Afterwards, Patricia and I went to a small café for lunch, but while we were waiting for our food, I picked up the local newspaper and found I couldn't read. I stared at the printed words without understanding their meaning and tried to tell Patricia, in garbled language, that we needed to return to the hospital. The doctor was alarmed at the rapid change and ordered an ambulance to take me to their neurological unit for surgery.

By eleven PM, I was wheeled into the operating room, where a half-dollar-sized section of my skull was removed to allow the accumulated blood to drain. Evidently that didn't work, and I returned to surgery two more times in the next couple of days.

Except for one bizarre episode, I was surprisingly tranquil. After returning from the second surgery, I fell into a paranoid state in which I was convinced the hospital was a prison. I decided to escape, so I removed the IV from my arm, grabbed the stand to use as a weapon, and ran through the ward and down four flights of stairs in my jockey shorts with two hefty male nurses in hot pursuit. They subsequently subdued me, returned me to my room, and tied my arms and legs to keep me from trying to escape again. About five o'clock in the morning, I discovered my cell phone within reach under the sheet and, with one finger, managed to dial Patricia's number.

When she answered, I asked, "Sweetheart, am I in a hospital?"

"Yes, you are."

When I explained the events of the night, I realized I'd been having a paranoid episode. The moment I identified my state of mind — which I had experienced before when enrolled in the government-sponsored study of LSD at Spring Grove Hospital — I began returning to normal.

Five minutes later, Patricia, who had been staying in a nearby hotel, stormed into the ward and demanded that the head nurse contact my surgeon and find out what drugs I was being fed.

The drug in question was Decadron, which was used to control swelling of the brain. Patricia un-holstered her iPad and within minutes found a long list of warnings and dreaded side effects of the drug. Halfway down the list of miscellaneous catastrophes was the caution: "May cause epic paranoia." Even in my confused state it was clear I was suffering from epic paranoia, and the surgeon agreed to suspend use of the drug.

By this time I had undergone three surgeries, the last a minor procedure to insert a drain. I was uncharacteristically calm throughout the entire process, sleepy but not anxious. One thing that helped me keep perspective was the skulls of Incas I had seen in museums who had been trepanned four or five times — evidently successfully — to purge evil spirits. If they had survived this "minor surgery," I had confidence that I would also. Thank God, the next morning when I woke, the little blood bottle around my neck was empty. The bleeding had stopped.

For the moment, it seemed I was on the mend and was free to leave the hospital. With quiet joy, we piled in the car and returned to Berkeley to a plethora of get-well cards, casseroles, cakes, and two hand-knit afghans.

GIF: It was at an ungodly hour on the Tuesday morning of June 24, 2008, soon after the wheels of my American Airlines jet touched down in Dallas, that I first learned you had suffered a brain hemorrhage and undergone two brain surgeries. For the previous two weeks, the family had been in Zacatecas, Mexico, staying with a local family and studying Spanish eight hours a day. But that's another story — the point is, my cell phone didn't work in Mexico, and it wasn't until we landed in Dallas that I was able to pick up the messages.

There were four voicemails from you, the last saying you'd undergone a second brain surgery that hadn't really worked. Surrounded by the noisy bustle of the airport, the cell-phone speaker tinny in my ear, your voice sounded slurred and exhausted. But, you assured me, you were fine, and I was not to worry.

Yeah, right.

I wanted to come to the Bay Area, but you put me off. It made me sad that you didn't want me with you. A few days later you got another surgery — as I understood it, they were basically drilling holes in your head to relieve the pressure — but really, you said, it was fine. No need for concern.

The following week, you told me you might have to undergo a more serious procedure — a craniotomy. In this operation, they would cut a fist-sized chunk out of your skull with the medical equivalent of a jigsaw so they could cauterize the offending blood vessels that were still leaking inside of your brain.

Ever since I'd heard your voice on my cell phone in Dallas, I'd been worried, uncertain what to do. When I heard about the possible craniotomy, I was afraid you might die and knew I would never forgive myself if I didn't come. I had to see you.

I arrived in San Francisco on July 17 at eight AM, rented a car, and fought my way through rush-hour traffic across the Bay Bridge into Berkeley. You'd asked me not to come to the house too early, so I stopped for a bite somewhere near Patricia's house. I was halfway through breakfast when my phone rang.

It was Patricia. You had taken a turn for the worse and were going immediately to the hospital. I threw a twenty on the table, ran out of the restaurant, and broke a dozen traffic laws getting to Patricia's place in the Berkeley hills. I rushed into the house, helped you into your car, and off we went.

I spent the next hour and a half sitting in the backseat of your shiny red Prius alternately making idle conversation and trying not to stare at your head. The doctors had shaved the hair on one side, done their work, then closed the incisions with a half a dozen shiny silver staples that looked like the half-inch construction staples I used to shoot out of a nail gun to put up siding. You looked like a bad parody of Frankenstein's monster. But aside from that, you seemed pretty normal. Actually you were a lot more relaxed than usual, and you spent much of the trip reassuring Patricia, telling her not to worry, helping her navigate the packed freeways, and patting her knee.

When we arrived at the hospital, Patricia let us off out front and went to find parking. You seemed at ease as we made our way into the waiting room. You joked with the nurses. You moved well, talked clearly, and appeared to be in a fine mood. I found myself wondering what the heck we were doing in the hospital. Eventually they wheeled you down the hall to give you the latest in a series of CAT scans.

After an hour or so the doctor showed up, and when Patricia asked if he could do the craniotomy today, he told us that he absolutely could. It would be a definitive solution. But he didn't seem in any hurry, so I started asking questions:

How often did this type of hemorrhage normalize on its own? (*Most of the time.*)

What was the danger associated with putting off the operation? (*Low.*)

What was the danger associated with the operation? (*It's pretty safe, but you never know what can happen when you cut into someone's brain.*)

And then the one that clinched it — what would you do if it were your father? (*I'd wait and see. Definitely.*)

We left that day without a craniotomy. I was relieved, Patricia was anxious, and you seemed almost indifferent: unconcerned about the operation, unperturbed about going home without it. You'd always seemed so afraid of death, so determined to not go gently into that good night, I was astonished and more than a little impressed by your calm stoicism.

The next morning I woke at Patricia's house in Berkeley after a restless night in a strange bed and went to the living room to meditate. Half an hour later you appeared, lumbering down the stairs like something from a zombie movie but in good spirits. We talked for a few minutes while you made tea and toast and put it on a tray so you could bring your wife breakfast in bed.

"This has been really difficult for Patricia," you told me over your shoulder as you ascended the stairs, balancing the tray. I was amazed and upset. Why, I wondered, wasn't she making you tea?

Over the next few days, my incredulity grew apace. The house phone seemed to ring four times an hour and your cell almost as frequently, often waking you. There were people in and out of the house all day, mostly members of Patricia's congregation, bringing food or good wishes or dropping by to offer their support, and you would always drag yourself out of bed and down the stairs to greet them. It was social city.

Each morning you got up early and repeated the ritual of bringing Patricia breakfast in bed. And each afternoon, I would drive you the short distance to a fire road in Tilden Park and accompany you on a walk. About the third day, I couldn't take it anymore.

"You shouldn't be here in Berkeley," I told you. "We should go to the farm in Sonoma so you can rest and relax, so you can be surrounded by quiet and beauty."

"No," you told me. "Patricia needs her support systems around her right now. It would be too hard for her in Sonoma."

"You're the one who had brain surgery," I burst out. "You should be recuperating, and with the phone ringing and people tramping in and out night and day, you can't even take a nap in peace."

You didn't get mad or even defensive. You stopped in the middle of the trail and just looked at me. Then you said, "Patricia is worried sick about me, and I want to do anything I can to make it easier for her. That's what I want; that's my decision, please respect it."

This was a serious conversation stopper. I mean, what do you say to that? For the next few days, I mulled it over. I was desperately worried about you. You weren't taking care of yourself. You were sacrificing your wellbeing, and jeopardizing your recovery, to support Patricia. That's how I saw it. I wanted to tell her to make you tea in the morning, then rip the phone out of the wall and board the front door shut. I wanted to kidnap you and take you to Sonoma, strap you to the bed, and force-feed you chicken soup and peppermint tea.

Once or twice, on our walks, I tried to broach the subject again, but you were completely clear about what you wanted. And finally I had to accept it. I still thought you were nuts, but you were a grown man, perfectly capable of making your own decisions, and utterly unambiguous about what you wanted.

Over the next week, as we waited for your next doctor's appointment, when Patricia was busy with church business, I tried to be available for conversation, food, walks in the afternoon — whatever you wanted. When she was home, I took long hikes so you could be alone with each other. I didn't completely give up on my agenda, but I pursued it on the sly. When you were napping, I snuck upstairs and turned your phone off. I met parishioners at the front door, thanked them politely for the food they invariably brought, then told them you were resting.

And strangely enough, by giving up my notions of how you should be acting and devoting myself to helping you pursue the path you had chosen, I came to a startling discovery.

You and I are very different in many essential ways.

In retrospect this epiphany seems so obvious, almost trivial, like, "Duh, what *did* you think?" I don't suppose I ever thought consciously, "I'm just like my dad in all the important ways." But I had somehow accepted it as so without having examined the assumption. And once I realized how different we were, I started looking a lot more closely at you. Instead of assuming I understood your actions — because your motivations would be the same as mine, because we were so similar — I came to the conclusion that in some ways, I didn't understand you at all, and even more profoundly, perhaps I never had!

Rather than creating a sense of alienation, this discovery opened worlds of possibility. During the next few days, I finally saw clearly how happy Patricia made you. How had I missed it before? I came to realize that you really did want all those people calling at all hours of the day and night, and that it was as much for your comfort as for Patricia's support. I saw that the act of bringing your wife tea in bed was a powerful symbol to you of normality, and that you did it at least as much for yourself as for her.

But these were, in the end, small realizations compared to the major shift they occasioned in my psyche.

**SAM:** Two days before my next doctor's appointment, with the specter of the craniotomy still hanging over our heads, you and I took a walk in Tilden Park. It was a warm day, and we strolled along a flat road that wound its way along a steep hillside through the deep shade of tall eucalyptus trees. For a while we talked about nothing worth remembering until we ran out of words and were engulfed in heavy silence. The accumulation of years of misunderstanding, of love mixed with irritation, the shadow of our fight at Pasqual's, left us reluctant to talk about the powerful emotions we were feeling.

I will always remember the moment your words shattered the silence like a bolt of lightning, accompanied by an epiphany.

"Dad, there is no other way to say this: Whatever it was I held against you all these years — the statute of limitations has run out."

It took a moment for me to understand what I had heard, and then a flood of gratitude rushed through the deepest channels of my psyche. I had not dared to think I would ever hear these words of forgiveness. The only words strong enough to match my emotions were the old religious ones: *conversion, born again, healed.* I felt like a sinner who had been forgiven, a prodigal father welcomed home by his son.

And yet there were ancient secrets and wounds that, for a long time, kept me from accepting the forgiveness and grace that were being offered me. I had never been able to confess to you the full measure of my betrayal and shame. My mind suddenly returned to a moment four decades earlier when I'd committed an act of betrayal for which I had never been able to forgive myself. I was standing on the beach in La Jolla with Heather, negotiating your future. We agreed Lael would remain with Heather in Prescott. But you were a problem.

"You have to take him," she said. "I can't handle him. He needs a father!"

"I can't," I said. "I'm living in a one-room apartment in Del Mar with Her. I have no place for him."

At that moment I felt you were a burden; you were standing in the way of my happiness.

I have seldom revisited that scene of betrayal, nor told anybody about it, because it forces me to confront my deepest shame. I abandoned you, and I still carried a burden of guilt. I numbed my sense of shame and sadness because I could not admit my loneliness was the result of my own actions. And now, all of a sudden, you had unilaterally declared that the statute of limitations had run out.

These days, when you are a grown man and I am growing old, I often find myself sitting on that rock again with Heather with the waves breaking all around. But this time I imagine myself saying, "I'll find some way to make it work; I want him with me."

**GIF:** And just like that, thirty-five years of guilt and blame dropped away. As the Buddhists say, "that karma was shed, never to return." The weird thing is that I didn't think about it beforehand; I didn't plan it. Like so many transcendent moments, this one passed without me really noticing, and it wasn't until later I understood the significance of what we had done that day.

In the end, you didn't get the craniotomy, and when we got the news you were going to be fine, Patricia let me take you up to Sonoma for a couple days — just the two of us. It was a remarkable sign of trust and a symbol of healing between her and me. And we had a great time, eating Thai food on the plaza, hanging out on the porch, and talking. After a few more days, when it was clear you were on the mend, I went home to Santa Fe.

Sometimes, I think knowing a person is overrated, and it is only acceptance of what we do not know that paradoxically allows us to see more deeply into another's soul. It wasn't until I let go of preconceptions about who you *were* that I was able to open my eyes and see what you *are* really like.

For so many years, I harbored sadness about how you'd treated me when I was a boy, and at the root of that grief was a fundamental inability to accept what you had done. I judged your actions by my values and found them unforgivable. It never occurred to me that your values, your circumstances, and your thoughts might be different from mine.

Again, this is obvious in retrospect — but so are most great discoveries once you see them.

And once I saw how different we were from each other, a great weight fell from my shoulders. I didn't understand what you had done. And I probably never would. What a relief. And suddenly those old twisted emotions seemed silly — you weren't that man, not now, maybe not ever.

And it was only through deep not-knowing that I was able to see that.

**SAM:** In the weeks that followed, we experienced a remarkable metamorphosis.

The more we talked, the more we found that our resolve to give up old narratives allowed us to discuss *anything*. Our new matter-of-fact honesty resulted in a decision to write a series of letters exploring the stories we had not shared. Declaring a statute of limitations created a level of trust that allowed us to tell the untold stories.

The result is this book.

# chapter 30

# Guilt, Sorrow, and Forgiveness

Forgiveness is the final form of love.

— Reinhold Niebuhr

**GIF:** In the early years, our relationship was like the Vietnam War. You were the Americans. There was no way I could stand against your military might — I was simply outgunned. Your razor intellect was a helicopter gunship I couldn't hope to fight from the ground. When I tried to dig in, you brought out the heavy artillery of righteousness and authority. And when all else failed, you scorched my jungle refuge with the napalm of your rage.

But I was the Vietcong. You could never pin me down or root me out. I dug pits of dishonesty for you to fall into, and planted the sharpened punji stakes of indolence in the ground. I buried landmines of malingering and sloth on the trails you traversed, waiting to explode the shaky image of your manhood with my cultivated inadequacies. I infiltrated the haven of your heart and struck you down with guilt from the only quarters you had believed yourself safe.

This dynamic created a self-perpetuating, negative feedback loop in which we were both perennially unkind to each other. Each of us felt ourselves to be a victim in this struggle which became justification for escalating atrocities — on both our parts.

From this perspective, it becomes very confusing to understand how either one of us was more liable or more innocent. But it is obvious that for such a negative feedback loop to continue, both parties must play their part. If either one recognizes the loop and refuses to participate, it is relatively easy to break the pattern.

But it has always been our oft-told myth that you were the villainous aggressor and I the innocent victim. This mythos was so familiar for so long that it disappeared from our psyches, yet all the time it exercised a tremendous power over us. Like a black hole, the gravity of that singularity grew so strong that light could not escape, and it became invisible, revealing itself to us only through a dense, impenetrable absence.

However, looking back at our struggles, it seems obvious that for many years I was a truly rotten kid. Your explosions weren't random or unprovoked. They were not unilateral acts of unwarranted cruelty, but rather the inevitable result of a constant, vindictive spiral of escalation in which I participated at least as much as you.

Yesterday morning, I went into Jasper's room to wish him a good day. He hopped up from the bed where he had been playing a video game, wrapped his arms around me, gave me a big hug, and said, "I love you so much, Dad. You're the best." And man, it lit me up like a thousand-watt bulb. That kind of affection and admiration from my son is one of the sweetest things I've ever known.

I never gave that to you.

All the time I was growing up, even before the divorce and doubly after, I criticized you and mocked you and accused you of hypocrisy. I withheld my love and denied you my approval. And I feel an abiding sorrow because of it. I know now how deeply this hurt you.

But perhaps you don't.

I never gave you the kind of affection that Jasper gives me until very late in the game, when the scars around those ancient injuries had hardened over. But if Jasper were to treat me the way I treated you, it would be unbearable. And no matter how poorly you and I got along when I was a boy, I know that you have always loved me as deeply as I do him, so I knew how painful this was. But you have never spoken about the wounds I inflicted or the pain I caused you.

Now this absence leaves me with an unfinished picture of your view of me. When I try to see myself through your eyes, there are huge blank spots on the canvas. When I look back on those years, from the perspective of being a father, it breaks my heart, and I find now that I crave your forgiveness for those childhood acts of cruelty. And I don't see how you can forgive me for wounds you cannot acknowledge.

**SAM:** It has always been difficult for me to acknowledge the negative feelings I had about you as a child. And now, so many years later, it is still hard to recognize the ways you were not a good son. But it is relatively easy to catalogue the ways you inflicted discomfort on me, the thorns you drove into my flesh:

As a little kid, you lied and exaggerated so much to overcome your sense of inadequacy that I couldn't tell when you were telling the truth;

As an adolescent you were a pain in the ass, with a gigantic attitude toward the world in general and your mother and me in particular;

You smoked too much dope;

Your malingering and resentment put me in a double bind. When I was critical of your negative attitudes, I was accused of being judgmental;

For a five-year period, every time I tried to take a picture, you flipped me the bird.

But these peccadilloes are symptoms that do not explain why during your extended adolescence, I frequently felt angry and had unkind thoughts about you.

**GIF:** I think that what continues to haunt you is not, at this point, primarily guilt for your actions as a father; but far more your inability to feel or understand how much our estrangement injured you — how deep and lasting those wounds have been.

It has been difficult for me as well to think about how cruel I was to you. But I want you to forgive me for the real cruelties I inflicted on you starting way back in the Kentucky years — not for relatively benign peccadilloes like flipping you the bird or smoking too much pot.

Should you say you forgive, but cannot recognize the depth of the wounds — the cruelty given and received — then the profession of forgiveness rings hollow.

**SAM:** Finally we get to the heart of the matter.

What I suffer from most is the vacuum — what *didn't* happen. When you tell me about the tenderness you share with your son, it sets up a sympathetic vibration in the heart of my being that is at once sorrow and longing for an intimacy that I did not have with you until recently.

There is:

a void where there should be a plenum of love,

an absence filled with you,

a wound and ache that never fully heals,

a sorrow that has no name,

a loneliness without an object.

I kept these feelings hidden because I didn't feel I had a right to be angry with you. If you screwed up, it was because I had been a rotten father. I felt I deserved your scorn, resentment, and rebellion. And more to boot. There was no way for me to pay off my account because the interaction between your blaming and my guilt kept the struggle alive.

Yes. I numbed myself so I would not have to feel the hurt or admit that you'd wounded me. I desperately and silently wanted you to love me, so I repressed the awareness of unloving feelings, yours and mine. I couldn't admit you broke my heart. I hoped in time you would forgive me, but it didn't occur to me that I would need to forgive you.

Now sorrow, longing, and forgiveness lie side by side in my soul.

I forgive you, as you have forgiven me.

The statute of limitations on all our trespasses has expired.

The circle of forgiveness is complete.

# chapter 31

# Gratitude

If the only prayer you said was thank you, that would be enough.

— Meister Eckhart

**GIF:** Yesterday I returned from a solo three-day backpacking trip in the mountains above Santa Fe. It was perfect late-fall weather: warm in the sun, the air crisp and cool in the shadows, with occasional biting winds. When I'm alone, high in the high country, my mind goes still. In one way, when I'm up there, I don't think much about anything — which can be a blessed relief, like a plunge into cool water on a hot day.

And yet, on another, deeper level, my mental perceptions become abnormally sharp, honed by solitude, the normal chatter of the daily grind stilled by the effort of carrying a pack for long hours over rough terrain. The profound quiet of the mountains allows me to hear my hidden thoughts, and the vast vistas of the high peaks provide a vantage point from which to overlook the landscape of my mind. Sometimes up there, it becomes inexplicably simple to navigate the twisted pathways of my own heart.

On this particular trip, as if drawn by some inner loadstone, I found my thoughts returning to you again and again. All through the three days, different images of you kept popping into my mind, conjured from the distant mists of recollection.

I remember . . .

. . . waking up on Sunday morning in Muir Beach to find you dancing around the living room wearing nothing but red bikini underwear and singing along to Hot Tuna, turned up loud on the stereo, in a strong, true baritone: "You know you rider gonna miss me when I'm gone."

Groggy from the night before, I'd said, "For God's sake, no one wants to see that — get a room." But looking back, I smile and shake my head at the sheer, raw, irrepressible joy of it.

. . . three days down the Paria Canyon in Utah with a whole group of backpackers, we came to a spot where the orange canyon walls were five hundred feet high, no more than ten feet across, and the water that filled the canyon from side to side had grown too deep to walk through. You stripped off your pack and most of your clothes and struck off swimming through the freezing water, not knowing how far it would be until you could stand. It turned out to be only fifty yards, and I remember how foolish you felt when Ann Galland blew up four Therm-a-Rest pads and paddled across to where you stood, staying dry and warm the whole way — but I always loved you for that foolish, thoughtless, brash courage.

. . . at a rest stop in the middle of nowhere in Arizona, when I was only six, you found a rattlesnake coiled behind a log. Convinced some unsuspecting soul would blunder on it and be bitten, you unpacked the whole car, produced (to my wonder) an old officer's pistol from WWII, and unloaded the whole clip at point-blank range — twelve rounds, all clean misses — then, a little sheepishly, killed the snake with a stick.

. . . me being lost and heartbroken at twenty-three, having left my cabin in Washington to pursue love, sleeping on friends' couches, staying at your house on weekends, picking up odd carpentry jobs, and saying to you one day, just in passing, "My friend Charles just applied to St. John's. He's smart, but not academically inclined, so it must be a remarkable place."

You said, "Let's fly out there tomorrow." And we did. I wonder often what path my life might have taken if you hadn't.

. . . hiking with you to the Tiger's Nest, a sacred monastery high in the Bhutanese Himalayas;

. . . climbing together in the Needles;

. . . snorkeling together in Hawaii with an ethereal Asian mermaid who beckoned to me (I know you thought it was you, but . . . ), inviting me into the deep.

But this time, for the first time, all these memories were imbued with a tremendous upwelling of affection and admiration.

I have loved you so much for so many years.

And until *now* — yes now, at fifty-four years of age — I have never felt it purely.

What's odd is that these were not "new" memories. Last year I could have recited the same events. But then they were tainted with regret, contaminated by cynicism. Each memory was interpreted through a lens of distrust, strained through a sieve of hurt.

And it was all because whenever I thought of you, whether I was conscious of it or not, I was always thinking first of the Egg and the Abandonment, the Log, the Bad Dream — all the oft-told mythic failings from our early years — and I interpreted all of my memories of you through this light. Or maybe I should say half-light.

And somehow, through some almost magical, alchemical process, by talking to you, and writing my stories, and reading your stories, those mythic events lost their primal stature. I no longer need to think of them in capital letters. They still hold a central place in my psyche — and probably always will — but they have taken on an appropriate size and importance. No longer are they the ONLY way I can remember you.

When this change occurred, it was as if these few stories had been a cork in the bottle of recollection. And when it was pulled, thousands of memories came flooding back — but this time instead of being in black and white, I saw you in the full range of Technicolor.

Dozens of scenes from building your house together swam unbidden into my mind — hundreds of incidents from childhood; from long-ago Christmases; from languid summers when I visited you in Del Mar, in Washington, in Muir Beach — all came pouring back.

And they were all filled with love and appreciation.

It was as if our entire past had been rewritten.

For those three days, as I walked in the high country, I reveled in you.

And I want to tell you now that I think you are a remarkable man. You always lived big, larger than life. You screwed up big, too — but that's only part of the story, the black-and-white part. You also gave me so much; we have shared so much, so much joy and pain and richness, so many wonderful moments. So much color.

And now I feel both sorrow and gratitude. Sorrow, because I wish I could have realized all this sooner, and profoundly grateful that we have had the opportunity to take this journey together and that I have had the chance to tell you all of this before you die.

# chapter 32

# Epilogue

For the son who has grown really to know the father,
the agonies of the ordeal are readily borne; the world is no longer a vale of tears
but a bliss-yielding, perpetual manifestation of the Presence.

— Joseph Campbell

Soon after we began to write this book, almost two years ago now, we realized we were inadvertently creating a new kind of initiation rite. We started by telling our stories — but not just any stories; we had to journey deep into the underworld of our pasts and dredge up the darkest, most radioactive memories of betrayal and injury that had stood between us. And there were many times when the stories revealed things we would much rather have kept secret.

We ventured into the unvisited chambers of our psyches and uncovered the old myths, which we had whispered over and over to ourselves for so many years that they became the only truth. And when they were exposed to light, they crumbled under their own weight and turned to dust.

We realized our relationship had been frozen since 1965. For almost half a century, whenever we were together, in the mythic theater of our unconscious, Gifford was forever eating that damn Sisyphean egg, humiliated and traumatized, while Sam was standing over him screaming, trapped in a frozen tableau of rage and shame.

No wonder we didn't know each other!

Whenever we were off on our own, away from each other, we lead rich, separate lives; we had adventures and families and jobs and became our own men. But whenever we came together, we were drawn into the same old steps — Sam, the guilty villain; Gif, the resentful victim. We were stuck in a familiar, unhappy landscape of black and white. Each of us knew exactly what was expected — that demon dance was ingrained into the muscle memory of our souls.

Within this context, nothing new could ever happen.

Then a miraculous thing occurred. Once we exhumed the tired, constricting stories of the past, dozens of new stories sprang unbidden from the archives of recollection. The new stories had their own logic of expansion — each one opened a fresh window on the world.

The process took on a life of its own, and to our surprise, the stories themselves rose up, rebelled against the tyranny of the oft-told myths, and killed the old stereotypes. The people we had been in those old stories died. Now they are gone and neither one of us can find them in our own hearts or in the other's eyes.

In tribal cultures, initiations were a ritualized way of passing from boyhood into manhood. By this process, a man came to know his place in the world, including how to be a father and a son. But we never had the benefit of those rituals. And since we lived so far from each other during these critical events, the rituals were not shared, and in a fundamental way, we never learned how to be a son and a father to each other. But writing this book, and the countless hours of conversations that have gone into it, have finally granted us the relationship we had always felt was our birthright but that we never knew how to claim.

This is a new type of initiation for a modern world where so many fathers and sons are separated by the exigencies of work and a culture that places disproportionate value on financial success. It suggests a process, a new set of rituals, by which we can deconstruct our myths and be initiated into a new understanding of what it means to be a father to a son and a son to a father in this scattered modern age.

Telling the stories and undergoing our shared initiation has changed us. It's not like we sit around holding hands and singing "Kumbaya"; we still argue — and we've had some doozies writing this book — but somehow the angry feelings that unexpectedly bubble (or explode) to the surface don't linger. They have lost their power. Now an angry exchange seems more like a thunderstorm, an act of our own capricious natures, that blows in unexpectedly and passes just as quickly, leaving the landscape refreshed and bright. We understand now that anger is simply a part of who we are, and that real dialogue is often a form of loving combat.

But now, even during times of conflict, the current of love runs unbroken, strong and swift. We both feel there is nothing pending, no unfinished business, no accounts to settle or issues to resolve.

As a result of pursuing this new form of initiation, we have finally come to understand the place we hold in each other's hearts. Our stories have told us in a way we never knew before how we belong together.

Gif had come to the farm so we could work face to face on polishing the book. At long last, we had come to the end. Exhausted from days of intensive effort, we decided to go out for dinner. It was while we were driving home up the narrow, dark road that leads to the farm that it happened.

There had been persistent rumors of mountain lions living in the area, probably in the tangled watershed of Agua Caliente just downstream from the farm. Ever since we'd built the house together a quarter of a century prior, we had talked about our near-obsessive desire to see a mountain lion. We were regularly blessed with sightings of bobcats, coyotes, and foxes, but never a mountain lion. For some strange reason, we felt we would not fully belong to the place we inhabited until we encountered our secretive feline neighbors. We often hiked in the hills and up volcanic cliffs that surrounded our small valley, armed only with stout staffs, searching out the most likely cat habitats. We found boneyards that provided evidence that our quest, although difficult, was possible. After all, it wasn't a unicorn or some unfeasible chimera we were looking for, only an elusive, perfectly normal (if numinous) mountain lion.

And suddenly there *they* were. Not one but two. When they first ran into the corridor of light cast by our headlights, we thought that they were foxes, then bobcats — but when their tails came into full view, it was clear they were adolescent lions. They looked strangely like giant replicas of Gifford's long-dead, orange-striped tabby cat. As they ran, loose-jointed, tumbling over each other in an effort to escape the light, their bodies had all the charm of kittens at play and the promise of adult power. When they reached a small hole in the fence and both tried to get through at the same time they, momentarily, became an undifferentiated ball of orange fur until they figured out they would have to take turns. We were hypnotized, wonderstruck, as they disappeared into the bushes.

After the initial excitement ebbed, we fell into silence. It was as if we had unexpectedly wandered into a long-awaited mythical time and space and had received a strange benediction. The epiphany of the lions seemed to cast a sacramental light over the struggles we had gone through, allowing the fullness of our love to come out of the shadows and show itself. Clearly, we had been blessed with an ending for our story more perfect than we could have imagined.

It was a moment for celebration.

# About the Authors

**SAM KEEN** was educated at Harvard and Princeton and was a professor of philosophy and religion. He was a contributing editor of *Psychology Today* for twenty years and is the author of the bestselling *Fire in the Belly* and a dozen other books. He co-produced an award-winning PBS documentary, *Faces of the Enemy.* When not writing or traveling around the world, he lectures and leads seminars on a wide range of topics. He lives on his farm in the hills above Sonoma, CA. www.samkeen.com

**GIFFORD KEEN** has a liberal-arts degree from St. John's College in Santa Fe and has worked in a variety of professions — from apple picker to software executive, from carpenter to real-estate investor. He describes himself as a retired software geek, reluctant landlord, and aspiring novelist. Gifford is the father of a teenage son and has a daughter in college. He lives with his wife in Santa Fe, NM, where he writes, meditates, practices yoga, and takes long walks in the high country. www.amazon.com/author/giffordkeen

## ALSO FROM DIVINE ARTS

**THE SHAMAN & AYAHUASCA:** *Journeys to Sacred Realms*
**Don José Campos     2013 Nautilus Silver Medalist**

*"This remarkable book suggests a path back to understanding the profound healing and spiritual powers that are here for us in the plant world, reawakening our respect for the natural world, and thus for ourselves."*
—John Robbins, author of ***Diet for a New America***

**ONWARD & UPWARD:** *Reflections of a Joyful Life*
**Michael Wiese     2014 COVR Award Winner**

*"Onward & Upward is the memoir of a rare and wonderful man who has lived a truly extraordinary life. It's filled with Michael Wiese's adventures, his incredible journeys, and his interactions with amazing people."*
—John Robbins, author of ***Diet for a New America***

**RECIPES FOR A SACRED LIFE:**
*True Stories and a Few Miracles*
**Rivvy Neshama     2013 IPPY Gold Award Winner**

*"Neshama's stories are uplifting, witty, and wise: one can't go wrong with a recipe like that. The timeless wisdom she serves up is food for the soul."*
—***Publishers Weekly***

**SOPHIA—THE FEMININE FACE OF GOD:**
*Nine Heart Paths to Healing and Abundance*
**Karen Speerstra     2013 Nautilus Silver Medalist**

*"Karen Speerstra shows us most compellingly that when we open our hearts, we discover the wisdom of the Feminie all around us. A totally refreshing exploration and beautifully researched read."*
—Michael Cecil, author of ***Living at the Heart of Creation***

**THE JEWELED HIGHWAY:** *On the Quest for a Life of Meaning*
**Ralph White**

*"Ralph White's luminous memoirs embrace the spiritual sphere of multiple revelations and portray a love of Gaia, our planet, as perhaps no one has done before. If some modern revelation has appeared on our planet, Ralph has been there, not in control, but willing to participate and be affected. The Jeweled Highway is vital and alive and not constrained by ideology or political correctness. It is Dionysian, a voyage without a plan, a trust in serendipity, an appreciation of love over logic."*
—Thomas Moore, author of ***Care of the Soul***

DIVINE ARTS

**THE DIVINE ART OF DYING:** *How to Live Well While Dying*
**Karen Speerstra & Herbert Anderson, Foreword by Ira Byock, MD**

*"A magnificent achievement. The Divine Art of Dying is a moving and inspiring book about taking control of your life as it starts to come to a close."*
— Will Schwalbe, author of the *New York Times*-bestselling *The End of Your Life Book Club*

**LIVING BEYOND THE FIVE SENSES:**
*The Emergence of a Spiritual Being*
**Teresa L. DeCicco, PhD**

*"Teresa DeCicco articulates clearly and eloquently the age-old exploration of transformation, spirituality, and religion from an insider's perspective: as a woman who's experienced the richness of life beyond the five senses."*
—Lisa Wimberger, author of *New Beliefs, New Brain*

**FREE YOUR MIND:** *A Meditation Guide to Freedom and Happiness*
**Ajay Kapoor**

*"Free Your Mind goes beyond today's fashionable mindfulness movement by using our thinking, rather than simply noting it. Kapoor carefully shows us how to use our minds to break down our mental conditioning and become truly free."*
— Franz Metcalf, author of *What Would Buddha Do?*

**LIVING IN BALANCE:** *A Mindful Guide for Thriving in a Complex World*
**Joel & Michelle Levey, Foreword by His Holiness the Dalai Lama**

*"Joel and Michelle have constructed a text of sheer brilliance. Every page offers new insights and truth."*
—Caroline M. Myss, PhD, author of *Why People Don't Heal and How They Can* and *Anatomy of the Spirit*

**THE POWER OF I AM:** *Aligning the Chakras of Consciousness*
**Geoffrey Jowett**

*"Geof Jowett is a healer, mystic, and altogether a wonderful spiritual teacher. Science and Spirit mix beautifully with him."*
—James Van Praagh, author of the # 1 *New York Times* bestseller *Talking to Heaven*

1.800.833.5738   24 HOURS

## Celebrating the sacred in everyday life.

Divine Arts was founded to share some of the new and ancient knowledge that is rapidly emerging from the scientific, indigenous, and wisdom cultures of the world, and to present new voices that express eternal truths in innovative, accessible ways.

Although the Earth appears to be in a dark state of affairs, we have realized from the shifts in our own consciousness that millions of beings are seeking and finding a new and optimistic understanding of the nature of reality; and we are committed to sharing their evolving insights.

Our esteemed authors, masters, and teachers from around the world have come together from all spiritual practices to create Divine Arts books. Our unity comes in celebrating the sacredness of life and in having the intention that our work will assist in raising human consciousness and benefiting all sentient beings.

We trust that our work will serve you,
and we welcome your feedback.

Michael Wiese, *publisher*